SOME FOLKS FEEL THE RAIN

Dear Kaja —
May God be with you —
as your future unfolds —
Joy & Peace & Delight
from the Church Staff
and
Rev. Dr. [signature]

JAMES W. MOORE

SOME FOLKS FEEL the RAIN

Others Just Get Wet

DIMENSIONS
FOR LIVING
NASHVILLE

SOME FOLKS FEEL THE RAIN
OTHERS JUST GET WET

This book is printed on acid-free paper.

Library of Congress Cataloging-in-Publication Data

Moore, James W. (James Wendell), 1938-
    Some folks feel the rain : others just get wet / James W. Moore.
        p. cm.
    ISBN 0-687-07754-0 (alk. paper)
    1. Christian life. I. Title.
BV4501.2.M58154   1999
248.4—dc21   99-32837
                                                           CIP

Scripture quotations, unless otherwise indicated, are from the New Revised Standard Version Bible, copyright © 1989, by the Division of Christian Education of the National Council of the Churches of Christ in the United States of America.

Scripture quotations noted RSV are from the Revised Standard Version of the Bible, copyright 1946, 1952, 1971 by the Division of Christian Education of the National Council of the Churches of Christ in the USA. Used by permission.

The prayer on page 16 is from *Markings* by Dag Hammarskjöld, trans., Auden/Sjoberg. Translation Copyright © 1964 by Alfred A. Knopf, Inc., and Faber & Faber, Ltd. Reprinted by permission of Alfred A. Knopf, Inc.

The poem on page 129 is from the book *Full Esteem Ahead* © 1994 by Diane Loomans with Julia Loomans. Reprinted by permission of HJ Kramer, P.O. Box 1082, Tiburon, CA. All rights reserved.

To become a steward of the dream, a blue ribbon on every person in America by the year 2000 and the globe by 2004 (story on p. 42-43), creating respect and dignity among all people, call 1-800-887-8422, email ablueribbon@aol.com or www.blueribbons.com.

00 01 02 03 04 05 06 07 08 — 10 9 8 7 6 5 4

MANUFACTURED IN THE UNITED STATES OF AMERICA

For
James Dawson Moore

Contents

Introduction

Some Folks Feel the Rain . . . Others Just Get Wet

On September 23, 1930, early in the morning a baby boy was born in Albany, Georgia. At that moment, of course, his family had no way of knowing that this bouncing baby boy would grow up to become one of the most beloved and respected entertainers of all time. He had to triumph over numerous hardships and tragedies along the way, but he did it with style and grace.

When the boy was five years old, he became gravely ill and gradually began to lose his eyesight. By the age of seven he was completely blind. Undaunted, the boy soon learned Braille, and a few years later he began to develop his musical talent by learning to play the piano. When he was fifteen, he became an orphan. Think of that: He was blind, he was orphaned, and he was only fifteen years old. But despite all of that, he refused to give up and give in. He kept working with his music and developing his talent.

At age seventeen, he moved to Seattle where he organized a musical trio, and he began performing. In 1952, at the age of twenty-two, he signed a recording contract with Atlantic Records, and ultimately became a world-famous recording artist and performer. This man's name (of course) is Ray Charles. If you have ever seen Ray Charles perform, I'm sure you've noticed immediately his creative genius, his soulful energy, his heartfelt sensitivity, his joy in per-

9

forming the music. He and the music become one. The music seems to flow freely out of him, and it seems to come from deep, deep, within.

Once, Ray Charles was being interviewed on television by Bob Costas. Bob Costas said to him, "Ray, not too long ago I watched you perform two different concerts on successive nights, and in both concerts you sang your classic hit 'Georgia,' but each time you sang it, you did it differently."

Ray Charles replied, "That's right! Every time, I do it differently, because, you see, I don't learn music by notes. I just let it bubble out of my soul!"

Now, when I heard Ray Charles say that, my mind darted back to a conversation I had participated in a few years ago. A group of people were sitting around one evening after dinner, talking about the great music entertainers of our time, when someone said, "What is it about Ray Charles that makes him so special?" A man in the group gave an answer that I loved. He said, "Some folks feel the rain; others just get wet. Ray Charles feels the rain!"

Some folks feel the rain; others just get wet. What does that mean? It means that some folks are vividly aware of what's going on around them; they are tuned in, they are sensitive, receptive, responsive, they lead with their hearts, they feel the joy, and they triumph over the pain. But, sadly, many people today don't! They don't celebrate; they just cope. They don't enjoy; they just endure. They don't feel gratitude; they just gripe and grumble. They don't embrace life; they just stonewall through it.

Some folks feel the rain; others just get wet. In other words, some folks smell the roses; others complain about the thorns. Some folks bask in the glow of a beautiful sunset; others dread the darkness that will follow it. Some folks see our time on this earth as a gracious gift from God; others see it as an agonizing endurance test. Some folks seize the day and celebrate life; others just cope.

I remember the precise moment when I learned the difference between these two approaches, the difference between celebrating life and coping with life. I was in my middle year of seminary. It was the start of the fall semester. I had heard lots of horror stories about this new professor who had come to campus to teach us philosophy of religion. Dr. Williams was his name. He had come from the philosophy department at Ohio State, and he was known far and wide as an excellent teacher but also a stern, tough, unbending taskmaster.

When Dr. Williams handed out the syllabus outlining the course requirements, I couldn't believe my eyes. It called for an incredible amount of reading, a midterm and a final exam, four quizzes, a research project and six (count them) term papers. After class, I followed Dr. Williams to his office. (Seminary "middlers" are a lot like college sophomores: I thought I knew everything!) I planned to question Dr. Williams about his syllabus and all of those requirements, and to give him a piece of my mind.

I strode into his office. He could tell I was upset. In the most sarcastic tone I could muster, I said to him, "Dr. Williams, you do *realize* that we have other courses besides *yours*, don't you?"

He looked over the top of his glasses and said to me, "Mr. Moore, sit down!" Now, when a professor looks sternly over his glasses at you and says, "Mr. Moore, sit down," you know right away that you are in big trouble! Humbly I sat down and waited for the onslaught.

"Mr. Moore, are you concerned about these six papers that you have to write?" he asked.

"Yes, sir."

"Mr. Moore, are you going to be a pastor?"

"Yes, sir."

"Mr. Moore, are you aware of the fact that you are going to have to write a paper every week for the rest of your life?"

"Sir?"

"Well, out there in the parish they call it a *sermon,* and you've got to write one *every week for the rest of your life,* and I'm going to let you practice on me."

Then came the part that changed my life. Dr. Williams came around from behind his big desk. He took off those ominous-looking glasses and tossed them aside. He sat down beside me, and his tone softened: "You know, Jim [notice he didn't call me *Mr. Moore* this time], you may be going about this all wrong. Don't see these papers and tests as a chore to be done. See them as an opportunity to speak out . . . to say what's on your mind . . . to stand tall for what you believe. Every day, I talk to you; here's your chance to talk to me. Every day, I teach you; look at those papers and tests not as a burden or chore, but as your chance to teach *me.* It's really very simple," he said. "You can celebrate life or cope with life. You can live or vegetate. You can see everything that comes your way as an opportunity or as a burden." And then Dr. Williams said this: "When you get out of school and get in the pastorate, you have a crucial choice to make. Each week you can say, 'Oh God, I have to write a sermon!' Or you can say, 'Thank God, I get to write a sermon!' "

You know what Dr. Williams was saying to me? He was saying something that changed my life forever. He was saying, "Some folks feel the rain; others just get wet. Some folks smell the roses; others gripe about the thorns. Some folks embrace life; others just see it as an endurance test. But as for you, Jim, I want you to feel the rain, smell the roses, embrace and celebrate life!"

Dr. Williams was right because he was underscoring what the psalmist was trying to teach us long ago when he said, "This is the day that the LORD has made; let us rejoice and be glad in it" (Psalm 118:24). These magnificent words have been used for centuries as an appropriate call to worship, but they are so much more. They are also practical and dynamic words for daily living.

If you and I could repeat that verse at the beginning of each day (and really mean it), it would change our lives. This is the day that the Lord has made and given to me, as a gracious and precious gift; I will rejoice and be glad in it, and be thankful for it. To resent the day—or to waste the day or to corrupt the day or to curse the day—is sinful and destructive.

How is it with you right now? How are you doing? Are you feeling the rain or just getting wet? If we want to feel the rain and smell the roses and seize the day, there are three things we need. Let me outline them. Here's number one.

First of All, We Need a Sense of Gratitude

The difference between just making the best of life and making the most of life is a sense of gratitude. The difference between coping with life and celebrating life is a sense of gratitude. The difference between enduring life and embracing life is a sense of gratitude.

Not long ago, I received a beautiful letter from a good friend that says it all. Listen closely to these touching words:

Dear Jim: Something happened to my sister, my mother, and me that I think you'd like to know about. Last Monday afternoon, my precious four-year-old nephew became terribly ill and had to be rushed to the hospital by ambulance. Needless to say, we were all hysterical.

The doctors and nurses stabilized him and began running tests. They put us in a room to wait for the results with all the anxiety and dread you feel when something could be terribly wrong with someone you love.

We were all wringing our hands, thinking the worst, when an elderly woman, a maintenance worker, peeped in the door to see if the room needed cleaning. We said, "Hello! How are you?" Her response touched me deep down in my soul. She smiled and said, "I'm blessed, thank you. How are you?" We all said, "Fine," and as she backed out of the room, we all burst into tears realizing the lovely thing this lady had said.

It made us think and talk about how blessed we all are and how blessed our family has always been, and that God is with us and we can face anything. Talking like that together gave us all such comfort. Later, the doctors came in and told us that the baby would be fine, that there was nothing seriously wrong with him. You can only imagine how relieved and how thankful we were.

Jim, can you think of a more wonderful response to the question "How are you?" than "I'm blessed, thank you"? Hearing that sweet, radiant woman say that changed my life forever.

If we want to feel the rain and not just get wet, if we want to smell the roses and celebrate life, one of the best ways I know of to do that is to look around and see how blessed we are. A sense of gratitude is so important.

Second, We Need a Sense of Humor

Joy, laughter, and humor are a part of our Scripture and our Christian faith. It's helpful and healthy to laugh at ourselves and the little ironies of life.

Some years ago, Wilsie Martin was appointed as the pastor of a large metropolitan church in Los Angeles. He was honored to receive that prestigious appointment. On his first Sunday to preach, he arrived early. As he stood looking out his study window, he noticed an elderly woman with a walking cane trying to climb the steep front steps to the sanctuary doors. Wilsie Martin rushed out to help her. "Pardon me, ma'am, but could I assist you up these steps this morning?

"Oh that would be so kind of you," she answered.

Slowly, tediously, the two climbed together, moving up

the steps with great effort to the great doors of the sanctuary entrance. When they finally reached the top, the woman turned to Wilsie and said, "By the way, can you tell me who is preaching at my church this morning?"

"I surely can," came the reply. With his shoulders straight and his head thrown slightly back, he said, "Wilsie Martin is preaching at your church today."

"Oh," said the woman. "Then could you please help me back down the stairs!"

I like that story for two reasons: First, it's funny. But I like it even more for another reason, namely this: How do we know this story? The only way we *could* is because Wilsie Martin told it on himself! He was big enough to laugh at himself, big enough to not take himself too seriously. I'm convinced that our world would be a better place if we would all "lighten up" a bit. If we want to feel the rain and not just get wet, if we want to smell the roses and celebrate life, then we need a sense of gratitude and a sense of humor.

Third and Finally, We Need a Sense of Partnership with God

A few years ago, I bought a book that had been written by a minister from Montana named Robert Holmes. I love the title. It's called *Why Jesus Never Had Ulcers*. Robert Holmes points out that Jesus never had ulcers because he had his priorities straight. He knew what was important. He knew who he was, where he was going, and who was with him! He had a sense of mission, a sense of calling, a sense of meaning, a sense of purpose, and a sense of partnership with the Father.

Now, let me ask you to try something. If you will go into life today and every day saying over and over within yourself, *I am committed to God, and I have faith in God; I am a child of God; God is with me; I am God's partner; I am working with God and for God, and God is working through me,* it will turn your life around.

If you will take up that spirit of partnership with God, your life will be changed incredibly. It will change the way you work, the way you act, the way you speak, your tone of voice, the way you relate to others. It will change your outlook, your attitude, and your energy level, and life will be better for you because that's the way God meant it to be.

Dag Hammarskjöld, former secretary-general of the United Nations, said it wonderfully in his daily prayer:

> [O God,] Give us
> A pure heart
> That we may see Thee,
> A humble heart
> That we may hear Thee,
> A heart of love
> That we may serve Thee,
> A heart of faith
> That we may live Thee.

Well, how is it with you? Can you feel the rain? Can you smell the roses? Do you have a sense of gratitude, a sense of humor, and a sense of partnership with God?

1

Can You Feel the Strength to Keep on Believing When It's Hard?

When the Wind Is Taken Out of Our Sails

But Thomas (who was called the Twin), one of the twelve, was not with them when Jesus came. So the other disciples told him, "We have seen the Lord." But he said to them, "Unless I see the mark of the nails in his hands, and put my finger in the mark of the nails and my hand in his side, I will not believe."

A week later his disciples were again in the house, and Thomas was with them. Although the doors were shut, Jesus came and stood among them and said, "Peace be with you." Then he said to Thomas, "Put your finger here and see my hands. Reach out your hand and put it in my side. Do not doubt but believe." Thomas answered him, "My Lord and my God!" Jesus said to him, "Have you believed because you have seen me? Blessed are those who have not seen and yet have come to believe."

—John 20:24-29

At 9:02 A.M. on April 19, 1995, we in America took a blow to the heart. When that horrendous bomb went off at the Alfred P. Murrah Federal Building in Oklahoma City, killing and maiming hundreds of innocent people, including a number of children and babies, it sent shockwaves of fear and anger and sorrow across the nation and around the globe, making the world feel heartsick.

In the days that followed, many of us were glued to our

television sets, looking on in disbelief at those horrible scenes of carnage, watching in hope and in prayer the heroic efforts of rescue teams, and trying to sort out the full story of what happened—and how it could happen in the heartland of America. I was particularly touched by the interviews with the people of Oklahoma City, and especially those with the children. For example, one little seven-year-old boy was being interviewed by a reporter. The little boy's father was in the federal building at the time of the explosion and was still missing. The little boy talked about how much he missed his dad and how he wished his dad would come home at night. Then the reporter asked him what he was learning from all of this. The little seven-year-old boy said, "I know now what a second is."

"What do you mean?" asked the reporter.

And the little boy said, "One second you're here, and the next second you're gone."

It was late on a Monday night. I was watching CNN. A reporter was interviewing a little girl. She couldn't have been more than six or seven. She was sitting on the couch in the den of her home—her little legs dangling off the edge of the couch, not long enough to reach the floor yet. The reporters asked her how she felt about what had happened. She said, "I cry a lot..." (and even as she spoke, she kept wiping the tears out of the corners of her eyes with the heel of her hand). And then she said, "Those little babies.... They killed those little babies. I don't understand that." She said, "I think about it all the time, especially at night when I go to bed...and it's hard to go to sleep."

"Do you think you will ever get over this?" asked the reporter.

Again, wiping away the tears, she said, "I may get over it some day, but I think it's going to take a long, long time."

Sunday night after the explosion, I talked to my friend David Severe, a minister in Oklahoma City. As he spoke, his voice cracked a bit from the strain of physical and emotional exhaustion. St. Luke's United Methodist Church in Oklahoma City, located just ten blocks from the federal building, had immediately been converted into a trauma center. David and other ministers had rushed there at once and had been working virtually nonstop since the time of the bombing, trying to help those who were hurting. Around the clock, they had been there to counsel with people—those who were waiting anxiously for some word, and those who had already heard terrible words. David shared with me some miraculous stories.

He told about one man whose arm had been blown off and how the man, ignoring his own pain, forgot himself and was rushing through the building helping others get out to safety. David told about another man on the seventh floor at the time of the blast, who felt himself going down and then suddenly realized that he was on ground level. Think of that. He went down seven stories—a free-fall in an exploding building—and he walked away without a scratch... but then rushed back into the devastated building to help others who were not so lucky.

He told about a woman who was working at her computer. The computer flashed, and the woman instinctively pushed back away from it. Then came the huge explosion. Briefly she closed her eyes... just for a few seconds... and when she opened them, she looked and saw that her computer and her desk and half the building were gone, and she was sitting in her chair on a narrow ledge! She was saved only because she had pushed back a few inches.

David also described some of the horror stories we have all read about and seen played out on our TV screens—stories of death, and destruction, and indescribable heartache. But then David said something that touched me deep down in my soul. He said:

If those terrorists thought for one moment that they could shake and undermine our faith, they were wrong. If those terrorists thought for one moment that their cruel and hateful act would crush our spirit, they were wrong.

We are pulling together.

We are helping each other.

We are united as never before.

And God is with us as never before.

God is with us nearer than breathing.

God will bring us through this.

We believe that with all our hearts.

Listen! Doesn't that sound like something the disciples of Jesus might have said after that first Holy Week? For a moment there on Good Friday, the wind was taken out of their sails. It looked like evil and hate and cruelty had won. But then came Easter, then came Resurrection, then came new life, then came victory. And I can just imagine that later, the disciples might have said something like this: If those evil people who nailed Jesus to the cross thought for a moment that they could shake or undermine our faith, they were wrong. If they thought they could defeat us or crush our spirit, they were wrong. If they thought for a moment that they could take the wind out of our sails, they were wrong; because they just don't understand how strong our faith is, how strong our hope is, how strong our God is.

A pretty good illustration of how a Christian can (with the help of Christ) bounce back from the jaws of defeat is found in John 20. There, we find the story of Doubting Thomas. *Sesame Street* has its Oscar the Grouch. *Snow White and the Seven Dwarfs* have their Grumpy. Charlie Brown and the *Peanuts* kids have their Lucy. And the early disciples have their Doubting Thomas. As we might expect, it is Thomas who is the last of the disciples to believe the Resurrection, and then only after dramatic proof.

When the risen Lord first appeared to his followers, one man was missing: Doubting Thomas. The wind had been taken out of Thomas's sails. He was down for the count. He had seen the Crucifixion with his own eyes. Can't you see him walking gloomily through the dark streets of Jerusalem—all alone, brooding in solitude, tears streaming down his face, mourning the death of his Lord? Even when the other disciples come to tell him that they have seen the risen Christ—that they have *talked* to him—Thomas just can't believe it. He doesn't have the energy to believe it. The wind has been knocked out of his sails. He is worn, he is tired, he is skeptical.

But then look what happens. The risen Lord comes to Thomas. He senses his problem. He hears his doubts, and he still loves him. Jesus understands Thomas's need, and he meets it. "Thomas, come and touch me. Put your finger here on my pierced hands. Reach out and feel my wounded side. Don't be scared anymore. Just trust me! Believe in me!"

Thomas falls down before Jesus and cries, "My Lord and my God," and a few days later he probably said something like this: "If those people who crucified Jesus thought for a moment that they could shake us or crush us or squelch our faith, they were wrong."

Now, let's "go to school" on Doubting Thomas. What can we learn from his experience that can help us when life threatens to take the wind out of our sails? Why was it so hard at first for Thomas to believe and hang in there? Let me list three ideas that speak to this, and I'm sure you will think of others.

Thomas Had Trouble Believing at First Because He Was a Dropout

This is indeed a big problem for many people. They drop out of the church. They quit. They run away. They detach themselves from the fellowship of believers. They pull back from their faith-support group, and, as a result, malignant tentacles of doubt creep in. Look at Thomas. Christ came to the disciples, to the church community, that night in the upper room. He startled them, surprised them, renewed them, resurrected them. But Thomas missed out simply because he was not there! Thomas missed it because he was *absent*. What about us? How many great moments have we missed out on because we weren't there in church?

Pastors love this part of the story. When we want to dramatize and underscore the importance of church attendance, the importance of the church fellowship, the significance of being involved in the church, we like to point to Thomas and say, "Look at that! Look at what Thomas missed because he had dropped out." He missed the miracle. He missed the moment. He missed the risen Christ—simply because he wasn't there, because he had dropped out of the church, because he had detached himself from the fellowship of believers.

Why do people doubt? Why do they have trouble believing? Why do they have a hard time hanging in there? There are many reasons, of course, but often it is simply that they have dropped out of the church. They are living in a moral fog, a state of confusion and uncertainty because they have lost their support system.

Now, let me say something to you with all the feeling I have in my heart: Please don't let that happen to you! Please don't drop out! Don't lose your church! Don't cut yourself off from the roots of faith! If you are in church, please *stay there!* If you have somehow dropped out or slipped away or just gotten out of the habit, please *come back!* Or if you have never really gotten into the church, there's no better time than now. We want you, and we welcome you with open arms. But more than that, God wants you and welcomes you with open arms.

That's the first thought I put down. Some, like Thomas, have a hard time believing at first, and they have a hard time hanging in there because they have dropped out of the church.

Thomas Had Trouble Believing at First Because He Mistakenly Assumed That the Only Truth Is Scientific Truth

The real truth is that the things we value most cannot be proved in a scientific laboratory. Scientific methods are valuable, to be sure, but they are not the only road to truth. In my opinion, the most important truths cannot be scientifically documented. The love of a woman for a man and a man for a woman, you can't put that under a microscope, but I believe it's real. The warmth a mother feels for her child, you can't really examine that with a magnifying glass, but I believe it's real.

Honesty, courage, penitence, forgiveness, morality, love, faith, goodness, humility, grace, self-sacrifice, commitment, mercy, loyalty, compassion, kindness. These can't be put in a test tube, and yet they are the things that matter most, and they represent the greatest truths in the world. Please don't misunderstand me. I am not knocking scientific truth, or the scientific method. I am all for it. All truth is God's truth. I am simply saying that there is a special brand of truth and reality that cannot be contained or observed in a laboratory.

Remember how Jesus said it to Thomas, "Have you believed because you have seen me? Blessed are those who have not seen and yet have come to believe" (John 20:29). Thomas had a hard time at first because he was a dropout, and because he mistakenly assumed that the only truth is scientific truth. That brings us to a third and final thought.

Thomas Had Trouble Believing at First Because He Thought Death Was the End of Life

Thomas had not experienced the good news of Easter yet, the good news that Christ has conquered death and through faith in him, we can have that victory too.

No picture has captured the tragedy and the heartbreak of the Oklahoma City disaster like that of the firefighter carrying the little baby girl. Baylee Almon was her name. The day before the bombing, little Baylee had celebrated her first birthday. In an interview, her mother, fighting through her indescribable grief, spoke through tears telling reporters that the only way she could make it, the only thing that keeps her going, is knowing that Baylee is in heaven now with God, and God will take care of her.

For the Christian, death is not the end of life. It is simply moving through a door called "death" into a new dimension of life with God. Recently, I received a letter from a good friend. His mother had died, and after her funeral someone had sent him a copy of Henry Van Dyke's *Parable of Immortality*. It meant a lot to my friend, and he shared it with me. The great writer Henry Van Dyke, reflecting on the meaning of death and immortality, writes

I am standing on the seashore. A ship at my side spreads her white sails to the morning breeze and starts for the blue ocean. She is an object of beauty and strength, and I stand and watch until at last she hangs like a speck of white cloud just where the sea and sky come down to mingle with each other. Then someone at my side says, "There she goes!"

"Gone where?" Gone from my sight—that is all. She is just as large in mast and hull and span as she was when she left my sight and just as able to bear her load of living freight to the place of destination. Her diminished size is in me, not in her. And just at the moment when someone at my side says, "There she goes!" there are other eyes—watching her coming and other voices ready to take up the glad shout, "Here she comes! Here she comes!" on the other shore.

This is the good news of our Christian faith, the message of Easter. When we commit our lives to Christ, God will always be there for us, even on the other side of the grave. So when life takes the wind out of our sails, we can sail on because God will send the strong breeze of his Holy Spirit to lift us and carry us and see us through.

2

Can You Feel the Zest of Life?

The "Prison Shuffle"

But we have this treasure in clay jars, so that it may be made clear that this extraordinary power belongs to God and does not come from us. We are afflicted in every way, but not crushed; perplexed, but not driven to despair; persecuted, but not forsaken; struck down, but not destroyed; always carrying in the body the death of Jesus, so that the life of Jesus may also be made visible in our bodies. For while we live, we are always being given up to death for Jesus' sake, so that the life of Jesus may be made visible in our mortal flesh. So death is at work in us, but life in you.

—2 Corinthians 4:7-12

You may be familiar with the name Charles Colson. Charles Colson is a native of Boston, and he holds degrees from Brown University and George Washington University. In 1969 Colson left a lucrative law practice to serve the nation as special counsel to President Richard Nixon. From 1969 to 1973, Charles Colson was one of the five men closest to President Nixon during one of the greatest governmental crimes in the history of the United States. We now refer to that crisis as the Watergate scandal.

At that time, Charles Colson was described as the White House "hatchet man." He was called tough, cold, tenacious, wily, and nasty. This former Marine captain supposedly had once boasted that he would run over his own grandmother to reelect the President. Because of his involvement in Watergate, Charles Colson was tried, convicted, and sent to prison. That awful experience was the "two-by-four" he needed to finally get his attention, and it led to his spiritual rebirth.

In December of 1973, this headline grabbed national attention: "Colson Makes Decision for Christ!" The story jarred Washington and puzzled many across America. Many suspected a gimmick. There was much skepticism, much unbelieving laughter, much bewilderment, lots of snickering and gossip and crude jokes. But, it was true. Charles Colson had indeed accepted Christ as the Lord and Savior of his life. Charles Colson had indeed become a devout and committed Christian. Charles Colson had indeed been "born again."

When Colson went to prison to serve his Watergate sentence, he noticed something that intrigued him. He called it the "prison shuffle": jailed people trudging along, just doing their time; jailed people plodding along, who had thrown in the towel and quit on life; jailed people hobbling along with bowed heads, slumped shoulders, and broken spirits; jailed people lumbering along, apathetic and bitter, defeated and disillusioned; jailed people moping along, with lethargic legs and sluggish souls.

Colson noticed that these inmates who do the prison shuffle try their best to blend into the woodwork or fade into the landscape. They want to mind their own business, to do nothing that calls attention to themselves. They don't want to get involved with anything or anybody. So, they just do the prison shuffle.

In this book *Born Again*, Charles Colson describes it like this:

Federal Prison Camp.... Two hundred and fifty men lived here, but watching them through the window was like watching a silent movie in slow motion. Droop-shouldered, sticklike figures of men were drifting aimlessly and slowly in the open area; others were propped up against the buildings and a few sitting in small clusters on benches. The figures just seemed to be floating ever so slowly. I was soon to learn that no one walks fast in prison.

[Everything was drab even] the expressions on the faces. *Something strange here.* Then it struck me—*no one was smiling.*... A chill swept over me.

(Fleming H. Revell Co., 1976; p. 266)

Today, Charles Colson is out of prison. He is living near Washington, D.C., and is serving as chairman of Prison Fellowship, a ministry he founded in 1976. The purpose of Prison Fellowship is to equip and assist the church in bringing "the good news of Christ" to prisoners, former prisoners, their victims, and their families. In other words, their mission is to help people move from the drabness of the prison shuffle to the joy of the Christian walk.

Now, interestingly, it's important to recognize that the prison shuffle is not confined to the penitentiary. There are people all around us (indeed, maybe some of us) who are not physically in jail but still are spiritually doing the prison shuffle. There is no spring in their step anymore, no zip, no zest, no life, no joy. Just dull, gray drabness. They have quit on life. They are just "doing time," just going through the motions. They are spiritually frozen, paralyzed, congealed. They are not "feeling" the rain, they are just getting wet!

Gail Godwin, in her book *The Finishing School,* describes it like this:

There are two kinds of people.... One kind, you can tell just by looking at them at what point they congealed into their final selves. It might be a...*nice* [enough] self, but you know you can expect no more surprises from it. Whereas, the other kind keep moving, changing.... They are *fluid.* They keep moving forward and making new trysts with life, and the motion of it keeps them young. In my opinion, they are the only people who are still alive. You must be constantly on your guard...against congealing.

(Viking Penguin, 1984; p. 4)

Some years ago, Simon & Garfunkel recorded a song that became a big hit all over America. It was called "I Am a Rock." The lyrics speak of a person who has, for whatever reason, become completely isolated and cut off from the rest of humanity and the world. This person says, "I have no need of friendship; friendship causes pain. It's laughter and it's loving I disdain." The speaker goes on to suggest that it was the disappointment of failed love that caused a change in mind-set, this resolve to be like a rock, feeling no pain, and like an island, cut off and apart from everything and everyone else.

When I first heard that song (although I like Simon & Garfunkel), I wondered: Are people hearing these words? Are they really hearing the sadness, the disillusionment, the coldness, the tragedy, the heartache in these words? See what this is saying: Don't bother me. I don't want to get involved with you or with anything or with anybody. I have quit on love and life and friendship and responsibility. I'm going to just do my time and look out for number one. I don't want to be connected to anybody. I'm a rock. I'm an island. Or in other words, I'm doing the prison shuffle.

Let me bring this closer to home and show you some ways (if we are not careful) this can play out in our own lives.

First of All, Some People Do the "Prison Shuffle" in Their Faith Pilgrimage

Christ came to bring us abundant life, radiant life, full life, meaningful, zestful life—and yet the truth is that so many people miss it. They give up and give in to the prison shuffle in their faith pilgrimage. They don't stand tall and walk each day with confidence and strength; no, they limp along, hobble along, mope along, doing the prison shuffle.

Let me show you what I mean. When Maxie Dunnam was pastor of Christ United Methodist Church in Memphis, he was driving down Poplar Avenue near his church one day when he came up behind a very expensive sports car with a strange bumper sticker. It read "I Am a Generic Christian." As luck would have it, the man driving the sports car soon turned into a car wash. Maxie Dunnam was so curious about that bumper sticker that he pulled into the car wash behind the man and asked him about the meaning of his bumper sticker. "What is a 'Generic Christian,' anyway?" Maxie asked him. The man replied, "Well, I want to go to heaven, so of course I want to be a Christian, but I don't want to get involved in any congregation or any denomination or any specific church or group or label. I just call myself a 'Generic Christian.'"

Reflecting on that experience, Maxie Dunnam said, "I wonder if we don't have too many 'generic' Christians and not enough disciples." In his own way, the man in the sports car who called himself a "generic" Christian was doing the prison shuffle in his faith pilgrimage. "I don't want to get involved...just minding my own business...just doing my time...blending into the woodwork...don't expect anything from me...I'm a 'generic' Christian...." Or in other words, "I'm doing the prison shuffle in my spiritual life."

Recently, I read about a woman who was talking to her pastor one day. She pointed out to him that he was constantly calling people "to draw near to God." Then she confessed that she didn't want to get close to God. She just wanted to get over in a corner and sneak into heaven quietly. She didn't want to be a saint, but she just didn't want to end up in hell.

The pastor was puzzled by her comment. She went on to explain that when she started into the ninth grade, she set her heart on finishing high school with straight C's and she did. She knew that if she failed she would have to repeat the year, and she wanted out, and she also knew that C's would do it. She was afraid that if she did too well, if she started making A's, people would begin to expect things of her. She told the pastor that the same is true with God. If you're too bad, you'll end up in hell, and she didn't want that. But, if you're too good, he'll send you to India, and she didn't want that either.

Isn't that sad? Isn't it a shame when someone—for whatever reason—becomes afraid to draw near to God? Afraid of the responsibilities, afraid of the expectations, afraid of the commitments—so they just throw in the towel. They give up and give in to the prison shuffle in their faith pilgrimage. That's number one.

Second, Some People Do the "Prison Shuffle" in Their Response to Hard Times

It is true that when hard times hit, one of the early stages of grief is a kind of "shocked numbness," which greatly resembles the prison shuffle. It's almost as if God anesthetizes us to get us through those first tough hours of anguish. "I can't believe this is happening to me," we cry, and we trudge around almost like zombies or like prisoners doing "hard time."

But God doesn't want us to stay that way. And if we will stay close to him, and trust him, and keep our faith in him, God will eventually bring us out of the valley to the mountaintop on the other side. He will deliver us from the prison shuffle of sorrow and enable us to stand tall and move forward with confidence and poise and strength.

Many years ago, a man hit rock bottom in his life. Hard times. Without warning, he lost his job. Just like that, for no apparent reason, he was fired; he found out later that the trickery of politics was the reason. He worked in a customhouse, a place where taxes and duties were paid by ships entering and leaving port. One morning he went to work and was told that his services were no longer needed; he was fired on the spot.

The man was absolutely devastated, defeated, humiliated. He didn't know how he could face anyone and let them know what had happened, especially his young wife. But when he shuffled home and told her, he was amazed by her response. She said, "Great! Now you can write your book. You've been wanting to write. Now's your chance!"

"I can't take time out to write," he said. "I've got to put food on the table for us."

But again she had a surprise for him. "No problem," she said. "I've been saving money every month for just such a time as this. And now, I have enough saved for us to live on for a whole year and then some."

And with that she opened up a drawer and there was a large sum of money she had hidden there! So, what did that man do? He took that time to write his book. (Oh, my, did he write!) And when that book was published, it eventually became one of the all-time best-selling classics in all of literature. The book was called *The Scarlet Letter,* and the man who wrote it was Nathaniel Hawthorne!

This brings to mind another writer, another man who wrote in hard times. He was called the apostle Paul. Listen to his words:

> We are afflicted in every way, but not crushed; perplexed, but not driven to despair; persecuted, but not forsaken; struck down, but not destroyed. . . .
> "Where, O death, is your victory?
> Where, O death, is your sting?"
> But thanks be to God, who gives us the victory through our Lord Jesus Christ.
> (2 Corinthians 4:8-9; 1 Corinthians 15:55, 57)

By the way, Paul was in prison facing hard times when he wrote those words. He had great faith in God, and because of that faith, he would not give up and give in to the prison shuffle. Sadly, though, many people today do. They do the prison shuffle in their faith pilgrimage and in their response to hard times.

Third and Finally, Some People Do the "Prison Shuffle" in Their Approach to Life

Over time, some folks do become disillusioned with life. They feel cheated and mistreated. They become bitter and jaded. So they cynically stonewall through their days. They give in to apathy and resignedly do the prison shuffle.

Have you heard about the young woman who was doing a survey? She asked a man this question: "Do you think lack of education and apathy are two of our biggest problems?" The man answered: "I don't know, and I don't care." But it doesn't have to be that way. The key to victorious living is found in this powerful passage in 2 Corinthians 4: "We are afflicted in every way, but not crushed... struck down, but not destroyed; always carrying in the body the death of Jesus, so that the life of Jesus may also be made visible in our bodies" (verses 8-10).

What does Paul mean? He means that through faith in Christ we can be victors; we can be saved; we can have new life; we can be set free. We don't have to do the prison shuffle. We can have a spring in our step and joy in our hearts, because when we open our hearts to Jesus Christ, nothing—not even death—can defeat us. He gives us the victory!

There is a delightful story about a man named Mr. Kline. "Old Man Kline" they called him. He was the town Scrooge. No one liked him. The adults told jokes about him, and the children made up derisive rhymes about Old Man Kline. Mr. Kline felt that life had dealt him a raw deal, and he was angry and bitter and selfish. One Sunday morning, Mr. Kline was feeling especially low—discouraged, defeated, and ready to end it all—when he walked by the church. The congregation was singing a hymn with these words: "Saved by grace alone, this is all my plea... Jesus died for all mankind, and Jesus died for me."

Mr. Kline's hearing was not too good, so when the congregation came to the words "Jesus died for all mankind," he misheard it and thought they were singing "Jesus died for Ol' Man Kline," and he exclaimed, "Why, that's me! That's *me!*" Mr. Kline stopped in his tracks. He went into the church. He heard the gospel of Jesus Christ, and he believed. He was born again. He became a new person. He didn't have to do the prison shuffle anymore. He could stand tall and walk now with joy and confidence. And so can we! So can we.

3

Can You Feel the Power of Commitment?

Limping Along When We Don't Have To

So Ahab sent to all the Israelites, and assembled the prophets at Mount Carmel. Elijah then came near to all the people, and said, "How long will you go limping with two different opinions? If the LORD is God, follow him; but if Baal, then follow him." The people did not answer him a word. Then Elijah said to the people, "I, even I only, am left a prophet of the LORD; but Baal's prophets number four hundred fifty."

—1 Kings 18:20-22

A while back, I had knee surgery. My old football knees had been screaming at me for some time (especially my left knee), so finally I swallowed my macho pride and went to see the doctor. The doctor took one look at my knee and the strange way I was walking, and he sent me over to the hospital for an MRI. The MRI revealed that I had a badly torn cartilage, some bone chips, and, as Dr. Bocell put it, "some other garbage in there that needs to come out."

So they scoped my left knee, and I went into the process of recovering. Most days I do pretty well. Some days, however, I do too much, walk too much, stand too much, climb too many stairs—and my knee gets angry with me and swells up defiantly. And when this happens, I find myself limping again, which is understandable. But, I have noticed something else that's very interesting: Sometimes I will start walking and suddenly realize that I'm limping when I don't have to anymore. I'm limping when it's not really necessary. I'm limping out of habit. I had limped along for so long that now, sometimes, unwittingly, I limp when I don't really need to. The torn cartilage has been repaired. The bone chips have been removed. The garbage has been cleaned out of my knee.

But still, sometimes I catch myself limping along, shuffling along, hobbling along, when it's not necessary anymore. It's just an old, bad habit that is hard to break. I had gotten so used to a bad situation that "limping" had become a part of my daily lifestyle. And now, I'm trying to unlearn that. Now, I'm trying to learn all over again how to stand tall and walk straight.

This situation reminds me of that powerful scene in 1 Kings 18 where the great prophet Elijah says to the people, "How long will you go limping with two different opinions? If the LORD is God, follow him; but if Baal, then follow him" (verse 21). What is this all about? Why did Elijah say that? What on earth is he talking about? Let me try to put it in context for us.

When the people of Israel came into the promised land of Canaan, they settled down beside their Canaanite neighbors. The people of Israel who had been wandering in the wilderness for many years (and had been slaves in Egypt for many years before that) now tried their hand at farming— and they didn't know the first thing about it. They had been nomads. The Canaanites, on the other hand, had been farming for many years. They knew how to do it. The Israelites had never farmed before at all. They were rookies at farming, totally inexperienced.

So, when the time came for that first harvest, who do you think had the best crops? Why, the Canaanites, of course, because they were experienced farmers. They knew what they were doing. They knew how to farm. The Israelites went over to their Canaanite neighbors and said,

"We notice that your crops are much better than ours. Why is that? How did you do it?"

"Simple," the Canaanites said, "wc prayed to Baal! He is our local fertility god, and we pray to him, and he gives us good crops."

Actually, Baal had nothing to do with it, but they *thought* he did. So, the Israelites began to wonder and reason like this: "We know God said to us, 'Have no other gods, and make no graven images.' We know we are supposed to worship God alone. But we sure would like to have better crops next year. Maybe if we prayed to Baal, just a little bit . . . what could it hurt? It might even give us a better harvest. Maybe it's worth a try."

But then along came the prophet Elijah. He saw what was happening, and he knew that it was wrong and hurtful and dangerous. He knew that this thinking and these actions were a violation of the Ten Commandments. He knew that Baal worship represented superstition and immorality and idolatry, and he knew he had to stand tall and speak out against this wrongful practice. Elijah also knew he had to do it powerfully, graphically, and convincingly. So he challenged the 450 prophets of Baal to a contest. The question was, Who is in charge of the universe? Is it God? Or is it Baal?

Elijah set up the contest. They piled up wood for a bonfire. Elijah then told the prophets of Baal to call on Baal to miraculously ignite the fire. For hours, the 450 prophets of Baal called out to their god, over and over again, but to no avail: Nothing happened. Elijah chided them, "Maybe you should cry louder. Maybe Baal has gone to sleep. Or maybe he is daydreaming right now. Or maybe he has gone on a trip" (1 Kings 18:27 paraphrased). By the way, the Scriptures tell us that those Canaanite prophets "limped around" their bonfire altar, crying out to Baal louder and louder, but no response, no answer, no fire. Finally, exhausted, they gave up.

Elijah then stepped forward to give it a try. To make the task more difficult and more awesome, Elijah asked that the bonfire wood be doused with water—not once, not twice, but three times! Then Elijah called on God to send fire from heaven—and immediately it came! The Scriptures describe it like this: "The fire of the LORD fell and consumed the burnt offering, the wood, the stones, and the dust, and even licked up the water that was in the trench. When all the people saw it, they fell on their faces and said, 'The LORD indeed is God; the LORD indeed is God'" (1 Kings 18:38-39).

In that ancient contest, the question Elijah put before the people of Israel is the same question we need to face today, namely this: "How long will you go limping with two different opinions? If the LORD is God, follow him; but if Baal, then follow him" (1 Kings 18:21). Some years before, Joshua had said the same thing to the people. He said it like this: "Serve [the LORD] in sincerity and in faithfulness; put away [false] gods. . . . Choose this day whom you will serve, . . . but as for me and my household, we will serve the LORD" (Joshua 24:14-15).

What a great thing for a father to say: "As for me and my house, we will serve the Lord." What a great thing for a mother to say, what a great thing for any individual Christian to say. "As for me and my house, we will serve the Lord." God comes first here. God is the Lord of life. We will stand tall and walk straight for him.

If we are going to stop limping around, and stand tall and walk straight for God and his church, there are several places where we can "put our weight down." Let me mention three of them.

First of All, We Can Walk in Love

If we want our children to stand tall and walk straight for God, one of the best things we can teach them is how to walk in love, how to go the way of love, how to choose the path of love. If we are not loving people, then spiritually we are limping through life. Being Christian and being loving are synonymous. Jesus called love the key sign of Christian discipleship.

There is a wonderful story that Thomas Wheeler tells. Thomas Wheeler is the chairman of the board of Massachusetts Mutual Life Insurance Company, and he tells how he and his wife were out driving in the country one day. He noticed that they were low on gas, so he pulled off at the first exit and came to a seedy, dilapidated little gas station with one pump. There was only one attendant working the place, so the executive pumped his own gas. But as he did so, he noticed that his wife was carrying on an animated, friendly conversation with the gas station man. When the two conversants saw Wheeler looking at them, the gas station attendant walked away, seemingly embarrassed.

Thomas Wheeler paid the man, and he and his wife drove away. As they moved out down the road, Wheeler asked his wife if she knew the gas station man. She said, "Know him? Indeed I do. We were very close in high school. We dated seriously and even talked of marriage."

Well, Thomas Wheeler could not help himself. He swelled up with pride, and he just had to brag a bit. "Boy, were you lucky I came along, because if you had married him you would be the wife of a man who pumps gas in an old dilapidated service station instead of the wife of the chairman of Mass Mutual."

To this his wife replied, "My dear, if I had married him, he would be the chairman of the board of Mass Mutual, and *you* would be pumping gas!"

That is a fun story, but it carries with it a serious point, namely that we are what we are because of our relationships. Change your relationships and your life is changed. We need to build our relationships on love—not envy, not jealousy, not competition, not vindictiveness, but love! We need to love people, and we need to tell them we love them. It's so important.

Helice Bridges, author and founder of Difference Makers International, a nonprofit educational foundation committed to providing school and community programs that create dignity and respect among all people, tells this story. Not long ago, a schoolteacher in New York called all of the children in her class forward and gave each one of them a blue ribbon imprinted with gold letters that read "Who I Am Makes A Big Difference." Then she told each student in turn what was special about each one of them and how each one made a big difference to her and to the class. To one student she said, "You have such a wonderful sense of humor, and you bring joy to our class." To another, she said, "You have such a curious mind, and you ask excellent questions that stretch our minds and help us grow." To still another, she said, "You are so kind to everyone, and your beautiful spirit inspires and encourages all of us" and on and on she went, praising each and every student.

The students were delighted. Then she gave the students some ribbons to take to other people out in the community and encourage them to do the same and keep it going. One student went to a junior executive who had helped him, and the junior executive in turn went in to see his boss, who had the reputation of being serious and grouchy. The junior executive sat down with his boss, told him about the project, and presented him with a blue ribbon. The junior executive said to his boss, "You are so brilliant! You have helped me so much, and you've taught me so much. You are a creative genius, and I appreciate and admire you more than words can express. You have made a big difference in my life, and I thank you."

The boss seemed very surprised. The junior executive pinned the blue ribbon on his boss, and then he asked the boss to take the extra ribbon and pass it on, to give it to someone who had made a big difference in his life. That night, the boss came home to his fourteen-year-old son and sat down with him. He said, "The most incredible thing happened to me today. I was in my office, and one of the junior executives came in and told me he admired me, and then he gave me a blue ribbon for being a creative genius. Imagine that. He thinks I'm a creative genius! Then he pinned the blue ribbon, which says 'Who I Am Makes a Big Difference,' on my jacket, just above my heart. He gave me this extra ribbon and asked me to find somebody else to honor.

"As I was driving home tonight, I started thinking about whom I would honor with this ribbon, and I thought about you. I want to honor you because you mean so much to me. My days are really hectic, and when I come home I don't pay a lot of attention to you. Sometimes I yell at you for not getting good grades in school and for your bedroom being a mess, but somehow, tonight...I just wanted to sit here and, well, just let you know that I love you so much and that you do make a big difference to me. You and your mother are the most precious persons in my life. You are great, and I love you!"

The startled boy started crying. He couldn't stop. His whole body shook. Finally, he caught his breath, looked up at his father, and said, through his tears, "Dad, I was planning to commit suicide tomorrow because I didn't think you loved me. Now I don't need to" (copyright © Helice Bridges of Difference Makers, Del Mar, California).

We don't have to limp through life. We can honor God by walking in love.

Second, We Can Walk in Trust

William Sloane Coffin once said that "faith is not believing without evidence, but trusting without reservation."

One night, a happily married couple were on a much anticipated trip to celebrate their twenty-fifth wedding anniversary, when their car slammed into a semi-trailer truck rig parked along the shoulder of the highway. They were both killed instantly in the grinding crash. Their three sons (ages twenty, seventeen, and sixteen) were left, in their grief, to open both anniversary cards and sympathy cards on the same day; to turn roses sent for a celebration into memorial flowers for a funeral; to take giant steps into adulthood by selecting caskets and burial spaces for their parents; and to cope with all the other details and decisions that are part of such a trauma.

The middle son, who handled most of the arrangements, testified how, in the wilderness of his confusion and grief, he had experienced more than once the powerful presence of God. He told his pastor that presently he saw God as his shelf, and although everything on that shelf had been moved around, changed or broken, the shelf had remained the same. He was discovering that the things he rests on the shelf will always change, but the shelf will not. Like the shelf, God is always the same.

God is always the same. We can count on that. And we can count on God! That son, though only seventeen, had already learned from his parents and his church how to trust God. Can you trust God like that? Are you limping along through life? Or have you learned how to walk in love and walk in trust?

Third and Finally, We Can Walk in Commitment

This is really what Elijah and Joshua were both talking about: commitment to God. They were saying, "Don't be so wishy-washy! Don't be so weak! Don't chase after every fad that comes along! Don't be so indecisive! Don't limp along through life unable to make a decision about God.

Choose this day whom you will serve. Commit every fiber of your being to God and his Kingdom."

Kara Newell expresses it well like this: "My mother is a potter and I've spent many happy hours watching her prepare the wet clay, plop a soggy lump of it on the wheel, start the wheel, and slowly draw the clay up into whatever form she has chosen. But, I've also watched her stop and start the process over and over when she's been unable to center the clay properly. [She knows that] whatever comes from uncentered clay will not be usable" (From "Executive Advice: Remarks by Senior Church Leaders" in *Christian Century* 110, no. 10, March 24-31, 1993; p. 322).

That's true for us too, isn't it? Unless we become clay in the Potter's hands and allow ourselves to be centered in him, we will not be useful in the ways that we are called to minister. We must learn how to center on God—how to commit to God. The point is clear: We don't have to limp through life. We can walk in *love*, we can walk in *trust*, and we can walk in *commitment*. Why go limping with two different kings? If God is God, follow him. Choose, this day, whom you will serve. But as for me and my house, we will serve the Lord.

4

Can You Feel the
Joy of Freedom?

Don't Turn Away

*"For it is as if a man, going on a journey, summoned his slaves
and entrusted his property to them; to one he gave five talents,
to another two, to another one, to each according to his ability.
Then he went away. The one who had received the five talents
went off at once and traded with them, and made five more talents. In the same way, the one who had the two talents made
two more talents. But the one who had received the one talent
went off and dug a hole in the ground and hid his master's
money."*

—Matthew 25:14-18

Shortly after we moved to Houston some years ago, a
good friend invited me to join him for lunch one day. The
restaurant he selected was at the top of a tall hotel building in Greenway Plaza. As we sat at a window table, we
were able to look down on the Compaq Center, the home
of the Houston Rockets. My friend picked that specific
place on that particular day because the circus had come to
town that morning, and we had a great view of the circus
animals being led off the train cars and into the Compaq
Center.

I was fascinated by the ways the circus people used the
elephants to do some of the work. Almost without effort,
those powerful elephants moved and carried some of the
heaviest equipment. But I was even more fascinated with

47

what the circus people did with the elephants after they finished their work. They secured the elephants by simply tying a rope around the back right leg of each elephant, and then tying the other end of the rope to a small wooden stake in the ground. Those elephants could easily have broken loose if they had tried, but they never even thought about it. They stood there completely immobilized by a single piece of rope and a small wooden stake.

My friend (who is a big circus fan) explained it like this. He said that "when an elephant is quite young, it is chained by the back right leg to an immovable stake, tethered by the back right leg to a stake set deep in concrete. For several weeks, the baby elephant does everything in its power to break free but cannot. Little by little, over time, the elephant is conditioned to believe that it can't move about freely when it is tied by the back right leg. As this conditioning process takes hold, you can tie the elephant with a string and it won't move. It doesn't move because it believes it can't. The chains in its mind are stronger than any man-made tether."

Something like this happened to the one-talent servant. He was immobilized, paralyzed, frozen by the chains in his mind, which told him he couldn't move in a new direction, he couldn't succeed, he couldn't try. When the master told him what to do, he froze up; he turned away; he buried his talent in the ground. Shackled by his own fear, he refused to even try.

This can happen to us as we move through life. We can become trapped, paralyzed, and frozen by chains in our minds. Let me show you what I mean.

First of All, We Can Be Frozen by Our Appetites

Dr. Harry Emerson Fosdick, when he was pastor of the Riverside Church in New York City, told a fascinating story one day about a vulture who was frozen and ultimately destroyed by his own appetites. It was a wintry day on the Niagara River below Buffalo, New York. This vulture (a bird of prey) had lighted on a carcass floating down the river, and he began to feed. He intended to feed on the carcass as long as he could and then to depart just before the rapids broke. He planned to feed right up to the last second, until just before the falls, and then break away and fly to safety into the sky.

But something happened that the vulture hadn't counted on. Moving swiftly toward the dangerous waterfalls, the vulture tried to fly away and escape—but he couldn't! He could not get away because on that cold, wintry day, his claws had frozen to the carcass he was feeding upon, and he was plunged over the falls to his death. He meant to break free at the last moment, but his talons were frozen. He was captured and destroyed by the clutch of his own claws!

Some time ago, a poignant thing happened. A young man broke into a convenience store, and then once inside, he called the police and asked them to come and arrest him. Why would he do that? Because he was addicted to crack cocaine. He had a $3,000 a week drug habit. He knew he had a big problem that was paralyzing him, a problem he could not handle alone, and this was the only way he knew to get help.

We can be frozen and immobilized and destroyed by our appetites. If we are self-centered, we are frozen to selfish egotism. If we feed on defeat, we are trapped in a prison of negativism. If we are hooked on alcohol or drugs or tranquilizers or food, we are locked in a spirit of escapism. If we constantly feed on jealousy or resentment, we are frozen in an iceberg of hatred. If we repeatedly say bad things about other people, we are crammed in a cage called gossip. If we always run scared—anxiety-ridden—we are frozen in a lifestyle of fear. And in every case, we are headed for a fall! We have lost our freedom.

The truth is that many people today are indeed slaves to their appetites; they do let one thing take control of their lives and immobilize them. Prejudice, envy, bad temper, worry, drugs, possessiveness—if we feed on things like that, we can be frozen in our tracks by our appetites. Listen! How is it with you? Is there one thing in your life that is enslaving you? The point is clear: We can be frozen by our appetites.

Second, We Can Be Frozen by Our Attitudes

A minister friend of mine tells a story about a woman who was a member of a church he served some years ago. Her name was Betty. The minister said Betty had the worst attitude he had ever encountered—always sullen, somber, cynical, sour, bitter, pessimistic. She was angry with life, against everything, and critical of everybody. The minister wondered why. He looked into it and discovered she had not always been like that. On the contrary, just a few years before, she had been quite the opposite: bright, happy, positive, energetic, optimistic.

He found out that five years earlier, a drunk driver had run his car up on the sidewalk and hit Betty's two-year-old daughter. The little girl was killed instantly, and Betty was devastated. In her grief, someone (who meant well) had said a terrible thing to Betty. Trying to explain the girl's death, someone said, "Betty, every now and then God gets tired of stale, worn-out flowers, and he wants a fresh, young rosebud for his bouquet."

My minister friend said that when he heard that, he understood why Betty was bitter and sullen, sad and cynical, and he was able to say to her, "Betty, don't you believe that for another minute. It was not God's will for your two-year-old daughter to die. It was not God's will that she be hit by a car. It happened because a man made a bad decision. He tried to drive while he was drunk. That's what did it, not God. God's heart was broken too."

Somehow that conversation with her minister touched a chord deep down in Betty's soul. It thawed her frozen heart, and her attitude changed. She wasn't mad at God anymore. She wasn't angry with life anymore. Slowly but surely, she was able to move forward with her life, and she became a positive, protective, loving person again.

Here's the point: Our theology affects our attitudes. How we feel about God greatly affects how we feel about life. Jesus talked a lot about attitudes. The inner life was very important to him. That's why he said over and over things like this: "Don't be afraid! Don't be anxious! God loves you! God will always be with you! You can count on that! God is on your side!" Now, if you hear that, really *hear* that, and believe it, it will change your attitude. It will make you a happier, more confident person. It will make you more productive and more optimistic. But that story has a strong warning for us—that we can be frozen by our destructive appetites and by our negative attitudes.

Finally, We Can Be Frozen by Our Anxieties

The one-talent servant refused to try because he was afraid. Afraid to act. His fears immobilized him, so he did nothing.

Remember the story about the man who went to the doctor because he was tired and run down all the time? The doctor checked him over and said, "The best thing you can do is stop drinking, go on a diet, start jogging, stop carousing around town every night!"

The man was thoughtful for a moment and then asked, "What's the next best thing?"

Isn't that the way most of us are? We feel ourselves getting caught in a trap and we want to break free, but we are afraid to pay the price, afraid to act.

Many of us know there is something we ought to do, but, like the one-talent servant, we are afraid to act, afraid to try, afraid to commit. I'm thinking of the father who knows he needs to spend more time with his children but somehow never gets around to it. I'm thinking of the person who has a broken relationship, who is estranged from another person. He knows it ought to be set right, but he is afraid to try. I'm thinking of the married couple who know the communication is breaking down in their marriage, but they just let it go and continue to drift apart. I'm thinking of those persons who ought to come on and join the church, but they continue to put it off. I'm thinking of those people who have dropped out of the church, who know they need to come back, but somehow they are afraid, afraid to act, and they are imprisoned and frozen by their fears.

Well, what's the answer? How do we get thawed out and set free? Christ sets us free by showing us that love casts out fear!

A few years ago in Marburg, Germany, an incident happened that illustrates the power of love to set us free. A young mother took her little daughter to the circus. All of a sudden, the child slipped away from her mother and disappeared. Picture the mother's horror when she saw that her child had somehow squeezed through the bars of the lion's cage—and there she was, right beside those ferocious lions! Already the claws were near the child.

Without a moment's hesitation, the mother rushed to the door of the cage, threw open the door, and charged in among the lions. She grabbed the child up in her arms, brought her out of the cage, and slammed the door in the face of the pursuing lions and then she promptly fainted! (Alan Walker, *Jesus the Liberator*, Abingdon Press, 1973; p. 22).

Now, that woman feared those lions as much as you or I would. But, she is a mother! And her love for her endangered child cast out any sense of fear she might have had and sent her to do something, a risky, dangerous something, that she would have thought impossible for her to do. The point is obvious: Love is the freeing agent. Love is the thawing agent.

When love is strong enough, you can be sure it will cast out fear and bring you out of whatever imprisons you. Love sets us free from our destructive appetites, negative attitudes, and crippling anxieties. And love lets us be God's children and God's disciples in the world. So don't become tethered by negative appetites and negative attitudes and negative anxieties, but instead, seize life and celebrate it to the fullest.

Can You Feel the Power of Love?

The Miracle of Love

One day Peter and John were going up to the temple at the hour of prayer, at three o'clock in the afternoon. And a man lame from birth was being carried in. People would lay him daily at the gate of the temple called the Beautiful Gate so that he could ask for alms from those entering the temple. When he saw Peter and John about to go into the temple, he asked them for alms. Peter looked intently at him, as did John, and said, "Look at us." And he fixed his attention on them, expecting to receive something from them. But Peter said, "I have no silver or gold, but what I have I give you; in the name of Jesus Christ of Nazareth, stand up and walk." And he took him by the right hand and raised him up; and immediately his feet and ankles were made strong. Jumping up, he stood and began to walk, and he entered the temple with them, walking and leaping and praising God. All the people saw him walking and praising God, and they recognized him as the one who used to sit and ask for alms at the Beautiful Gate of the temple; and they were filled with wonder and amazement at what had happened to him.

—Acts 3:1-10

Their names were Bob and Karen. They had just moved into their new dream home. Theirs was the first home completed in the new subdivision that was being developed in a beautiful wilderness area, some twenty minutes from downtown. They would soon have lots of neighbors, as other houses were going up all around them. But at the moment, they were the only residents in the new development.

Bob had rushed off to work after breakfast. Karen had straightened the kitchen a bit, and as she turned away from the sink, she could not believe what she was seeing: a five-foot-long snake was slithering across the kitchen floor, heading toward the living room. All of her life, Karen had been morbidly afraid of snakes, deathly afraid of snakes!

Her husband had gone to work. There were no neighbors around to help her. For a brief moment, she was absolutely petrified, frozen, paralyzed with fear, but she knew she had to act. She knew she had to do something. So she prayed, "O dear God, please help me!" Quickly, into her mind came a Bible verse she had learned as a child in Sunday school: "I can do all things through Christ who strengthens me."

Suddenly, Karen sprang into action. She grabbed a large paper grocery bag from the kitchen corner. She knew that what she was about to do was risky and dangerous, but courageously, she did it. (Now, as they say, don't try this at home, but here's what Karen did.) She caught up with the snake in the middle of the living room. She carefully and cautiously placed the open paper bag in front of the snake's rapidly flickering tongue. Then she touched the snake's tail with an old cane. Amazingly, the snake immediately went inside the bag. Karen instantly grabbed the top of the bag, raced outside, and threw it as far as she could. Then she dashed back inside, slammed the door, locked it, and called 911, and then she called her husband. When they all arrived, Karen told them what she had done, and then she promptly fainted!

Later, Karen's husband referred to what she had done as a "miracle of love." Why did he say that? Why did he call her courageous action a miracle of love? Well, you will understand more clearly when you hear the rest of the story. You see, Karen was not alone in her new home that morning when that five-foot-long snake came calling. Asleep in the nursery was her new two-month-old baby girl, and the snake was heading toward the nursery when Karen corralled him in the paper bag.

Where did Karen find the strength to do something she never would have believed she could do? Where did she find the courage? It came from the presence of God, from the encouragement of the Scriptures, and, yes, from the power of love. Karen's husband Bob was right. It was indeed a miracle of love. The Bible is full of "love miracles" like that. When Jesus healed blind Bartimaeus, it was a miracle of love. When he converted Zacchaeus, it was a miracle of love. When he went to the cross for you and me, it was a miracle of love. And when he came out of the tomb, it was a miracle of love.

And that's what we see in Acts 3:1-10. Here we see the miraculous healing of the man who can't walk, who is asking for money or food at the beautiful gate of the Temple. It was indeed a miracle of love.

In the musical *Go Out Singing,* written by Bill Heyer and composed by Hank Beebe, this is one of the most wonderful scenes in the play. Here's the context: Pentecost has just happened. The Holy Spirit has come. And now Peter and John are going up to the Temple when they see this man, who is unable to walk, and in the play this conversation takes place:

"Peter, why don't you give it a try?" John asks.

Peter replies, "Give what a try?"

"The Lord said, 'Look after my flock.' Give it a try," says John.

"Oh, John, come on, you know I can't perform a miracle," Peter begs.

Then John urges, "Peter...give it a try. What will it hurt? Try. Go ahead."

Peter walks very reluctantly to the man who is unable to

walk. Embarrassed, he stands over him, and with great hesitancy he stammers. "Um...uh...um, oh, in the name of Jesus Christ of Nazareth, I uh...I uh...bid you, rise and walk." The man stares up at Peter as if Peter were crazy. Peter stares back with diminishing hope. Finally, Peter breaks, turns, and walks downstage. Peter looks upward with embarrassment and says, "Oh, forgive me, Master. I've overstepped my bounds. I know this was a stupid thing to do. What was I thinking? I'm no good without you. I'm so sorry. How foolish of me. Please forgive me for even thinking I could..."

Now, while Peter is saying all of that, behind him the man is getting up on his feet, testing his legs, and then he shouts, "Look! I can walk! I can walk! I can walk!" Instantly confident, Peter looks back at him and says, "*Of course* you can!" Then (in the musical), Peter and the man break into a magnificent song and dance, a soft-shoe routine called "Praise, Praise the Lord," with the man, who only moments before could not even walk, dancing all over the stage, bringing down the house.

At the conclusion of that number, someone says to the man, "Look at you! Walking! What a wonder! What a marvel! What a miracle! You! Walking!"

The man replies, "And there's something even more wondrous and more marvelous?"

"What's that?"

He says, "I didn't know I could dance!"

This is a serendipity. The man was looking for alms, for money, yet he got something different. Something better. "I have no silver or gold, but what I have I give you; in the name of Jesus Christ of Nazareth, stand up and walk." And he does.

This is one of the most fascinating love miracles of the Scriptures, because it not only records Jesus' healing of a person with considerable physical and social challenges, but it also suggests that we too (through the grace of God) can be miracle workers. When we act in the name of Jesus, when we live in the spirit of Christ, *we* can be miracle workers too. Jesus put it strongly in the Gospel of John (14:12) when he said, "Very truly, I tell to you, the one who believes in me will also do the works that I do and, in fact, will do greater works than these."

Let me ask you a question. If you had the power right now to perform one miracle, what would it be? What would you do? The way we would answer that question would reveal a lot about us, wouldn't it? Now, with that as a backdrop, let's look together at three possibilities. Here is number one.

First, We Can (With the Help of God) Be Miracle Workers with Our Words

Recently, I have been thinking about my own life and wondering what in the world would have happened to me had it not been for certain people who came along to give me just the right words at just the right time—words that turned my life around, works that picked me up when I was down, words that gave me new life.

I remember my first sermon, preached at St. Mark's Methodist Church in Memphis. I was a tenth grader, sixteen years old. I got up in the pulpit and read the scripture lesson. I preached all the way from Genesis to Revelation and drank three glasses of water in four minutes. Four minutes, and it was over!

Now, I know some people *like* four-minute sermons, but I felt awful—embarrassed, defeated, humiliated, ashamed. And during that last hymn, I thought, *This is not for me. I can't do this. I'll never try this again!* But then after the service, one of the older saints of the church, Mr. Carter, came up and shook my hand, and with a warm smile he said, "Son, you did just fine! You did really well! I'm so proud of you! I think you've got the makings of a minister, and I believe God's gonna make a preacher out of you."

Now, as I think back on that moment, I know that Mr. Carter was probably just feeling sorry for me, but I will always be grateful to him for giving me the right words at the right time. It was a miracle what those words did for me. Those words picked me up, lifted me up, inspired me, and made me want to try again. We can work love miracles for one another with our words.

Second, We Can (With the Help of God) Be Miracle Workers with Our Attitudes

I have seen it many times: The attitude of one person can change the whole atmosphere of a place. An office, a class, a neighborhood, a church, a family; the whole situation can be changed, redeemed, made better by the influence of one person.

Some months ago, we helped a young woman in our church get a job. After she had been in that new position for about a month, her boss called to take me to lunch, and he said, "I want to talk to you about that young woman you sent to us last month."

I was worried, and asked, "Is she not working out?"

And he replied, "Oh, no, just the opposite. She is great! I wanted to tell you [and these were his words], she has absolutely worked a miracle in my office. The whole attitude has changed. She is a ray of sunshine. It is unbelievable what she's done, and I wanted to thank you for sending her to us!"

We can be miracle workers with our words and with our attitudes.

Third, We Can (With the Help of God) Be Miracle Workers with Our Actions

In the spring of 1887, Helen Keller was a deaf and blind girl who was terrifying to those around her. She uttered unintelligible, animal-like sounds and in a rage she would smash dishes and throw herself on the floor in frightening temper tantrums. The conclusion of many was that seven-year-old Helen Keller was an idiot, and that the situation was hopeless and there wasn't much reason to doubt that conclusion.

But then Anne Sullivan came into little Helen's life. Anne Sullivan, a twenty-year-old tutor, arrived at the Keller home in Tuscumbia, Alabama, to be Helen Keller's teacher. For weeks and weeks, she got nowhere. She tried and tried to break through by spelling words into Helen's hands, but with no luck. Finally, on April 5, a break-through occurred. At the well house, Helen was holding a mug under a spout. Anne Sullivan pumped water into the mug, and when the water poured onto Helen's hand, she continued to spell "w-a-t-e-r" into Helen's other hand.

Suddenly, Helen understood! The lightbulb turned on! She grabbed Anne's ever-ready hand and begged her for more words. A new world had opened for Helen, and she flourished in it. Anne Sullivan spent most of her life with Helen Keller. She went to college with Helen, sitting by her throughout every class at Radcliffe. Helen went on to become the friend of kings and princes and an inspiration to the whole world. All because of the actions of a young twenty-year-old teacher who would not quit, who would not give up, and who kept on loving and caring for her pupil when it seemed so hopeless.

Later, when a play was written about Anne Sullivan's work with Helen Keller, do you remember what they called it? That's right: *The Miracle Worker!* A perfect title, because Anne's actions with God's help worked a miracle.

We can be miracle workers with our words, our attitudes and our actions.

Please remember this. When Peter healed the man (Acts 3:1-10), he did it "in the name of Jesus Christ." "In the name of Jesus Christ, stand up and walk," he said. Now that phrase "in the name of Jesus" means "in the spirit of Jesus," and the message is clear. When we act in the name of Jesus Christ, when we live in the spirit of Jesus Christ, we can do incredible, amazing things. When we live in the spirit, we can be miracle workers with our words, with our attitudes, and with our actions.

6

Can You Feel the Strength to Persevere?

We Don't Have to Reinvent the Wheel

When they had finished breakfast, Jesus said to Simon Peter, "Simon son of John, do you love me more than these?" He said to him, "Yes, Lord; you know that I love you." Jesus said to him, "Feed my lambs." A second time he said to him, "Simon son of John, do you love me?" He said to him, "Yes, Lord; you know that I love you." Jesus said to him, "Tend my sheep." He said to him the third time, "Simon son of John, do you love me?" Peter felt hurt because he said to him the third time, "Do you love me?" And he said to him, "Lord, you know everything; you know that I love you." Jesus said to him, "Feed my sheep. Very truly, I tell you, when you were younger, you used to fasten your own belt and to go wherever you wished. But when you grow old, you will stretch out your hands, and someone else will fasten a belt around you and take you where you do not wish to go." (He said this to indicate the kind of death by which he would glorify God.) After this he said to him, "Follow me."

—John 21:15-19

Several years ago, when Darrell Royal was the head coach of the Texas Longhorns football team, he was known all across the country, not only as a highly successful football coach, but also as the "King of the One-liners." In his down-home style, he could cut to the heart of things and sum them up pretty quickly in a simple, folksy sound bite statement or comment. Probably his most famous one-liner came before a Cotton Bowl game some years ago.

Coach Royal's Texas Longhorns had won the Southwest Conference title and had reached the Cotton Bowl by using their vaunted run-oriented, wishbone offense. Coach Royal was not fond of the passing game and used to say, "When you throw the ball, three things can happen—and two of them are bad!" So, he liked to run the ball. However, just a few days before the Cotton Bowl, a sports reporter pointed out to Darrell Royal that the team they would be facing on New Year's Day was number one in the nation in defense against the run.

Then the reporter asked Coach Royal if the other team's great defensive record against the run would cause the Longhorns to change their style and pass the ball more. I love Darrell Royal's now-famous one-liner answer. He said, "You dance with the one who brung you!" Now, with all due respect and apologies to the English teachers of the world, I have to say that while Coach Royal's grammar could use a little work, nevertheless, his point was directly on target. What did he mean by that—"You dance with the one who 'brung' you"? In his homespun way, Coach Royal was saying, "You don't change horses in the middle of the stream"; "You don't abandon ship just because a storm has kicked up"; "You play your game and stay with your strength"; "You stay with the tried and true"; "You stay with what got you this far"; "You don't have to reinvent the wheel!"

Strange as this may sound, this reminds me of the Scripture in John 21, the post-Resurrection appearance of Christ on the seashore, where he cooks breakfast for the disciples (verses 4-14) and then has that touching conversation with Simon Peter. The risen Lord says, "Look, Simon Peter, if you really love me, then just feed my sheep." Three times, Jesus says it: "If you love me, take care of business: feed my sheep." Or in other words, "If you love me," then "hang in there!" "Stay with it!" "Keep it going!" "Don't change horses in the middle of the stream!" "Don't jump ship on me!" "Don't abandon the plan!" "Don't revert to the old life!" "Hold the flock together!" "Don't reinvent the wheel!" "Take up my torch!" "Dance with the one who 'brung' you!" "Don't chase after every new fad that comes along, and don't be thrown for a loop by every wind that blows. Just follow me!"

Now, that was great counsel for Simon Peter. It was just what he needed to hear, and these are great words for us today. Let me show you what I mean with three thoughts.

First of All, We Don't Have to Reinvent the Wheel When It Comes to Church Attendance

The one who "brung" us showed us in his words and in his actions that it is so important to keep the flock together and spiritually fed; that it's so important to support the church with our prayers, our presence, our gifts, and our service.

There's a great story about Stuart Henry, Professor Emeritus at Duke University. He taught American Christianity there for many years. Dr. Henry was walking across the Duke campus one Sunday morning, and the bells in the chapel tower were ringing loudly up ahead. He was dressed up in his Sunday best, and he was walking briskly, as if not to be late for the opening of the service.

A student saw him and said, "Hi, there, Dr. Henry. Did you decide that you would go to church this morning?"

Stuart Henry kept walking and said, "No, I didn't decide to do that this morning."

The student looked puzzled. "Oh, I'm sorry," he said. "I could have sworn you were going to chapel."

"I am," Dr. Henry said, "but I didn't decide to go this morning."

The student, somewhat baffled, said, "Oh, I don't guess I understand."

And Dr. Henry said in reply, "Look, son, I didn't make the decision to go to church this morning. I made that decision more than fifty years ago when I first became a Christian. So, it is never a decision whether I'll go to church, but only a decision where I'll go to church" (From a sermon by Norman Neaves, "Settle It Once and for All," October 30, 1994).

Some years ago, a young couple came to see me. They were having marital problems—getting into a big argument every weekend over whether or not they would go to church. The first weekend back home from their honeymoon, the wife had said, "Let's go to church Sunday." The husband thought to himself, "I don't want to be henpecked," so he rebelled and refused to go. They argued all weekend.

The next weekend the husband, feeling guilty about the way he had reacted the week before, said: "Hey, let's go to church Sunday." To this, his wife replied, "No way! You wouldn't go with me last Sunday, I'm not going with you this Sunday!" Again they fussed and fought all weekend. Week after week this happened. Every Friday, the tension would begin to crackle in the air, and soon they were fighting again about whether or not to go to church on Sunday. It broke my heart to hear their story, to think about how they were fussing and fighting over church.

Finally, I said to them, "You know, we never have that argument at our house."

"What do you mean?" they said.

"Well, we just decided in our family a long time ago that we go to church on Sunday. We made that decision one time. We don't have to reinvent the wheel on that every weekend. We go to church. Decision made! It saves a lot of time and energy."

"But that's different," they said, "you're the minister! You have to go!"

"Wait a minute," I said to them. "Think about that. Is it

different, really? I know thousands and thousands of committed Christian laypeople who never argue about whether or not they will go to church. They don't even discuss it. They have already made that decision, one time, years ago: *We go to church. We support the church. We stand with the church. No excuses! No question! No discussion! We will be there!*"

In every generation there are always some false prophets who try to dupe us with their slick words. They tell us church attendance is not as important now as it used to be. But they are so wrong! If it were right to attend church and support the church ten years ago, fifty years ago, one thousand years ago, it's right now. If Jesus were physically present here with us today, I believe he would say to us, "Hang in there!" "Don't jump ship!" "Don't run away!" "Stay with the plan!" "Keep the flock together!" "Feed my sheep!" "Support the church!"

The point is clear: "We don't have to reinvent the wheel when it comes to church attendance."

Second, We Don't Have to Reinvent the Wheel When It Comes to Morality

In every generation, there are always those who try to confuse us and trick us with regard to morality. They tell us that times have changed and therefore morality has changed. They say, "Those things we used to consider wrong and sinful aren't really so bad after all. So don't be an old stick-in-the-mud. Be modern, be hip, be with it. Everybody's doing it, so come on and join in."

Why do they do this? Why do they try to dupe us and pull us into their shady (and sometimes even sordid) lifestyles? Is it to ease their own guilt? Or is it because they operate under the mistaken notion that if enough people do it, then that makes it all right? Well, let me tell you something. Killing and stealing were wrong ten years ago, fifty years ago, and two thousand years ago, and they are wrong now! Lying and cheating were wrong ten years ago, fifty years ago, and two thousand years ago, and they are wrong now! Hurting and hating were wrong ten years ago, fifty years ago, and two thousand years ago, and they are wrong now!

We ought to thank God every day for the Ten Commandments, because they tell us how things are, how things work, how life holds together, how God meant things to be. The Ten Commandments are *not* the ten suggestions! They represent our spiritual and moral roots. They are the unshakable, unchanging, spiritual laws of God, and they are just as dependable today as ever. They are just as certain today as the Law of Gravity. When we violate them, somebody gets hurt. It's as simple as that. Thank God for the Ten Commandments, and thank God that Jesus took us a step further by showing us that love is the fulfillment of the law! He summed up the Ten Commandments in one great commandment: Love God and love your neighbor (see Matthew 22:34-40).

Not long ago, I made an interesting discovery in the Bible that fascinated me. I was studying Paul's letter to the Colossians. In Colossians 3:15*a*, Paul says, "Let the peace of Christ rule in your hearts." I got interested in that word *rule.* "Let the peace of Christ rule in your hearts." I went back to the original Greek text and found that the word translated *rule* is from the Greek word *Brabeneto.* I went then to the Greek lexicon and discovered that the word *brabeneto* is a word from the sports world. It means "umpire"! Think of that: Paul is saying, "Let the peace of Christ, the spirit of Christ, the love of Christ be the umpire in your soul and in your morality. That is, test everything by the measuring stick of love. Whenever you are trying to decide what to do, let love be the referee, the judge, the umpire."

In John 13:34-35, Jesus put it like this: "I give you a new

commandment, that you love one another. Just as I have loved you, you also should love one another. By this everyone will know that you are my disciples." We have the answer in our hands. We've had it all along. It's in the Book! So, we don't have to reinvent the wheel when it comes to church attendance, and we don't have to reinvent the wheel when it comes to morality.

Third, We Don't Have to Reinvent the Wheel When It Comes to Salvation

Every generation presents us with new fads, new movements, new temptations, new enticements. They promise a quick fix for our spiritual hunger and restlessness, and they threaten to pull us away from the one who really can save us. Please don't be taken in by these slick, false prophets who are here today and gone tomorrow. Stay with the one who has brought us this far! Trust the plan! Hold on tight to the Rock of Ages!

One day, a man decided to take a shortcut across a field. He fell into a deep pit. He tried his best to get out on his own strength, but he couldn't make it. He began to scream for help. He cried out for someone to save him. A pop psychologist passed by and said, "I feel your pain. I empathize with what you are going through down in that pit." A TV talk-show host came by and said, "When you get out—*if* you get out—you can come and be on my show." A religious fanatic happened along and said, "Obviously, you have sinned a great sin. Surely you have, because only bad people fall into pits."

A news reporter rushed out and asked, "Could I have an exclusive story on your experience in the pit?" A lawyer came out and wanted to represent the man in a lawsuit. An IRS agent came out to see if the man had paid his taxes on the pit. A neurotic came along and said, "You think *your* pit is bad; you should see *mine*!" An optimist said, "Things could be worse." A pessimist said, "Things will get worse." But then another person came along. He saw the man's dilemma, and his heart went out to him. He reached down with both hands, and, with strength and grace, he pulled the man up and out of the pit.

The man thanked his rescuer and then ran into town to tell everyone what had happened. "How did you get out?" they asked him.

"A man reached down and pulled me out," he said.

"Who was the man?"

"It was Jesus!"

"How do you know that?"

"I know it," he said, "because he had nail-prints in his hands!" (Thanks to Fred Craddock. See *Homiletics*, July-Sept. 1994; p. 13.)

You see, we *don't* have to reinvent the wheel. We can just take hold of those hands. We can just hang in there and trust the plan. We can stay with the tried and true. We can dance with the one who brought us. We don't have to reinvent the wheel when it comes to church attendance—when it comes to morality—and when it comes to salvation.

7

Can You Feel the Attitude of Gratitude?

Grit, Grace, and Gratitude

He entered Jericho and was passing through it. A man was there named Zacchaeus; he was a chief tax collector and was rich. He was trying to see who Jesus was, but on account of the crowd he could not, because he was short in stature. So he ran ahead and climbed a sycamore tree to see him, because he was going to pass that way. When Jesus came to the place, he looked up and said to him, "Zacchaeus, hurry and come down; for I must stay at your house today." So he hurried down and was happy to welcome him. All who saw it began to grumble and said, "He has gone to be the guest of one who is a sinner." Zacchaeus stood there and said to the Lord, "Look, half of my possessions, Lord, I will give to the poor; and if I have defrauded anyone of anything, I will pay back four times as much." Then Jesus said to him, "Today salvation has come to this house, because he too is a son of Abraham. For the Son of Man came to seek out and to save the lost."

—Luke 19:1-10

A few years ago, I received a fascinating letter from Larry Mathis. At that time, Larry was president and chief executive officer of the Methodist Hospital in Houston, and he is a member of our church. In his letter, Larry had included a remarkable essay. The essay had been written by David Saucier, a former patient at Methodist Hospital. As a matter of fact, David Saucier was only the fourth

71

patient at Methodist Hospital to receive a heart transplant.

The poignant essay had been written on the tenth anniversary of David's heart transplant operation, and it is entitled "Number Four Is Still Alive." Let me share some of this with you. Read carefully David Saucier's remarkable words as he reflects on his life after heart transplant surgery. He writes.

> Ten years ago in the wee hours of the morning of October 15, 1984, God performed a miracle in me. It was not the first miracle he had performed in my life, nor was it to be the last, but it was perhaps the most dramatic.
>
> The transplant team at Methodist Hospital under the leadership of Dr. Michael DeBakey performed their fourth heart transplant...replacing my damaged, doomed heart with one from a young man whose own life had tragically ended.
>
> Now, some may call this a miracle of modern science, but life itself is a miracle of God, and for another person's heart to grow to my severed aorta...and become a part of the living "me," is a miracle of God in my book!

David Saucier goes on to say

> Many people have asked me if I feel any different, or if I act any different, if the transplant has changed my life in any way. I can answer that in three ways:
>
> (1) First, there is urgency. I live with a renewed sense of urgency, and that has changed my priorities, because I realize that if I am to stop and smell the roses, I had best to do it now.
>
> (2) Second, there is gratitude. I don't understand [this miracle that has happened within me with my new heart]. All I can do is accept and feel grateful for each additional day I live.
>
> (3) A third change is that I now walk a little closer to God, because when you have been through a harrowing experi-

ence with someone, you form a special bond with them. Recovering from the transplant was at times a harrowing experience, and I guarantee you I clung to God for dear life during those times. He was the good friend who saw me through, sometimes the only one who thoroughly understood. I am grateful that he was there for me.

David Saucier concludes his essay with these words:

Deep, down inside I know that God will always take care of me. I also know that no one lives forever, and that someday he will decide he can better care for me on the other side of the Jordan. But, until that time, Number Four is still alive, and enjoying every minute of it.

David Saucier's words are pretty amazing. He is talking about a new lease on life, a new beginning, a new chance— all because he received a new heart. And that new heart gave him a fresh sense of urgency and gratitude and closeness to God.

Something like that happened to Zacchaeus. We find his remarkable story in Luke 19. Zacchaeus didn't have a heart transplant, but he did have a heart transformation. The Great Physician touched his heart and turned his life around.

Somewhere back there in the past, Zacchaeus had gotten off track. The children sing, "Zacchaeus was a wee little man, and a wee little man was he." Well, he was a "wee little man," all right, not only in physical stature but also in spirit.

Bad habits had taken root in Zacchaeus's heart. Greed, selfishness, the lust for power, prestige, and money had possessed him. And they were destroying him; Zacchaeus had a diseased heart, and his sick heart was cutting him off from other people and from God.

But then along came Jesus. And when Jesus touched his

heart, look what happened to Zacchaeus! We see in his experience the drama of redemption; the power of conversion; the miracle of the transformed heart.

When the light of Christ spilled into his life, Zacchaeus was exposed in all his littleness. Perhaps for the very first time, Zacchaeus saw himself as he really was: greedy; self-centered; a traitor, a cheat, a con man. And Zacchaeus didn't like what he saw. He was ashamed and penitent.

But he realized that help was available for his dark heart. Even after all he had done, he felt somehow that this man from Nazareth could help him. And he was changed. Talk about a conversion! By the miracle of grace, through the presence and love of Christ, his life was absolutely changed. Christ came into Zacchaeus's life and made him over.

• Don't miss the impact of this! Don't miss the message for your life now!

• If you are doing something you ought not to be doing.

• If you are possessed by some bad habit that is tearing you apart.

• If you are living a lifestyle that you are ashamed of...

• If you have somehow gotten away from God and the church.

• If your heart is not right with God.

• If you want to change.

God has the power to touch your heart and turn your life around. He can give you a new start, a new chance, a new beginning, a new lease on life, a new heart. It happened for Zacchaeus. It happened for David Saucier (the transplant patient). And it can happen for you and me.

But for this to happen, three things must come together—grit, grace, and gratitude. *Grit* is the courage to seize the moment; *grace* is the saving power of God's love; and *gratitude* is the spirit of appreciation and thanksgiving.

That's what the Zacchaeus story is about. Grit, grace, and gratitude. Let's take a look at these, one at a time.

First, There Is Grit

If you look up the word *grit* in *Roget's Thesaurus*, you will find these synonyms: guts, bravery, stamina, backbone, pluck, nettle, spunk, fortitude. The meaning of the word *grit* comes into even sharper focus when we look at its antonyms, its opposites: timidity, fearfulness, faintheartedness, cold feet. So for our purposes, let me define the word like this: *Grit* is the courage to sense and seize the moment.

We see some good examples of this in the Zacchaeus story. For one thing, Zacchaeus had the good sense to recognize that the coming of Jesus into Jericho that day was a special occasion. There was an urgency about it. Zacchaeus wanted to experience it firsthand. He wanted to see the Master. He wanted to seize the moment. But there was a huge crowd, and Zacchaeus was short. He couldn't see over the other people. But, he was determined. He had the grit to climb that sycamore tree, and it paid off. Oh, my, did it ever!

We also see the spirit of "true grit" in Jesus. When Jesus saw Zacchaeus up in that tree, his heart went out to him. Jesus sensed the loneliness of Zacchaeus, and he went over and reached out to this despised tax collector with love and acceptance.

Jesus knew full well that he would be criticized for associating with Zacchaeus. He knew that people would gripe and grumble and gossip and complain. But with grit, Jesus seized the moment—and he turned Zacchaeus's life around.

A few years ago, Mark Trotter told a beautiful story about a boy whose parents were missionaries to India. When the boy was twelve years old, his parents left him and his younger brother, and they went to India to start their tour of duty.

Their intention was that once they got settled they would send for the boys. But shortly after they left America, World War II broke out. They couldn't get to the boys, and they couldn't get the boys to them. The missionaries and their sons were separated for about eight years.

When the war was over, the parents returned to America. Their oldest son was twenty years old now and in college. He recalled how excited he was when he got word that his parents would soon arrive in their hometown by train.

The son got to the train depot early, even before the sun came up. When the train finally pulled in, the mother and father were the only ones who got off. The son wrote:

> I could barely see them in the haze, and they could hardly see me. We embraced in the semi-darkness. Then my mother took my hand and led me into the light of the waiting room. There were tears running down her cheeks as she looked at me. She kept looking at my face, staring hard. Then, she turned to my dad and called him by name. "Albert," she cried. "He's gone and looked just like you. He looks just like you."

This happened to Zacchaeus, spiritually. He came down out of that sycamore tree looking and sounding and acting like his Lord. Look at what he said. The very first thing he said was, "Lord, half of my goods, I will give to the poor."

Zacchaeus's greedy, selfish, diseased heart had been transformed. Now, he had the heart of love, the heart of compassion, the heart of generosity, the heart of his Lord— all because he had the courage, the guts, the grit to seize the moment. All because he had the backbone to accept this new heart Christ could give him.

How is it with you, right now? Do you need a new heart? Do you have the courage, the backbone, the grit to say yes to God? There are many people who truly want God to touch their hearts. They may even go in to church, ready to make a commitment to the Lord; but sadly, many of them will turn and walk away. They will put it off till another day, because they can't find the strength to do something about it. They can't find the fortitude to step forward. There are times when we all need grit—the courage to seize the moment.

Second, There Is Grace

The Zacchaeus story is jammed full of "Amazing Grace," the saving, healing, redemptive, life-changing power of God's love. In the early days of the Salvation Army, a young man named Alexander was made treasurer of the Army. William Booth, who was the founder of the Salvation Army, and his wife, Catherine, loved Alexander. They trusted him and treated him like a son.

Little by little, however, Alexander began taking money from the treasury. He took more and more until finally he was caught and arrested and sent to jail. William and Catherine still loved Alexander. They visited him in prison, wrote him letters weekly, and prayed for him daily.

Alexander was touched by their gracious spirit. He was penitent, and he asked for their forgiveness. On the morning Alexander was released from jail, Mrs. Booth was waiting outside the front gate of the prison with a little thermos of tea. She invited Alexander to sit down on a nearby bench, and then she poured him a cup of tea.

"Alexander," she said, "I have something here more than tea." She reached into her purse and pulled out a moneybag. "General Booth and I want you to come back to the Salvation Army and help us," she said to him. "And we want you to begin your duties as treasurer this very morning!"

Let me ask you something: Can *you* love like that? Can you forgive like that? That's what grace is. And that's the way God loves and forgives us. He is offering that kind of love and forgiveness to you and me right now. But we have to accept it. We have to have the grit to accept the grace.

First, there is grit, the courage to seize the moment; then, there is grace, the saving, life-changing power of God's love.

Third and Finally, There Is Gratitude

The spirit of appreciation and thanksgiving is so important. Thanksgiving is more than a national holiday. It is more than turkey and dressing and cranberry sauce. It is more than a day off from work and two days out of school. It is more than football games and family reunions.

Thanksgiving is a spirit that pervades the life of the Christian, day in and day out. It is the ongoing recognition of God's love for us. God's generosity toward us and his presence with us. Can you imagine the incredible gratitude that must have welled up in the soul of Zacchaeus that day when he felt the love of Christ touching his heart?

He felt loved and accepted and valued. So should we.

One of my favorite *Peanuts* comic strips is one that was printed some years ago, just a few days before Thanksgiving. Lucy is feeling sorry for herself, and she laments, "My life is a drag. I'm completely fed up. I've never felt so low in my life.'

Her little brother, Linus, tries to console her and says, "Lucy, when you're in a mood like this, you should try to think of things you have to be thankful for. In other words, count your blessings."

To that, Lucy says, "Ha! *That's* a good one! I could count my blessings on one finger! I've never had anything and I never will have anything. I don't get half the breaks that other people do. Nothing ever goes right for me! And you talk about counting blessings! You talk about being thankful! What do I have to be thankful for?"

Linus says "Well, for one thing, you have a little brother who loves you."

With that, Lucy runs and hugs little brother Linus as she cries tears of joy. And while she is hugging him tightly, Linus says, "Every now and then, I say the right thing." (See Robert Short, *The Gospel According to Peanuts*, John Knox Press, 1964; p. 23.)

Well, what about us? We have a God who loves us. And if that doesn't make us sing the song of thanksgiving, I don't know what would. That's what Zacchaeus realized that day in Jericho. He realized that God loved him, even *him*!

David Saucier, the heart transplant patient, said that his new heart gave him a new sense of urgency and gratitude and closeness to God. The same thing happened to Zacchaeus, and it can happen for you and me. But it takes grit, grace, and gratitude.

8

Can You Feel the Call to Discipleship?

When You Are Tired of Clapping with One Hand

As he was setting out on a journey, a man ran up and knelt before him, and asked him, "Good Teacher, what must I do to inherit eternal life?" Jesus said to him, "Why do you call me good? No one is good but God alone. You know the commandments: 'You shall not murder; You shall not commit adultery; You shall not steal; You shall not bear false witness; You shall not defraud; Honor your father and mother.'" He said to him, "Teacher, I have kept all these since my youth." Jesus, looking at him, loved him and said, "You lack one thing; go, sell what you own, and give the money to the poor, and you will have treasure in heaven; then come, follow me." When he heard this, he was shocked and went away grieving, for he had many possessions.
—Mark 10:17-22

Wealth, youth, and power! How in the world could you beat that combination? To be young, and to have the energy and drive to enjoy life to the fullest; and then, to have the money and means to pay for it, and the power to command respect as you do all of that. What a glorious existence that must be for the lucky few who manage to have wealth and youth and power all at the same time!

For most of us, that is a fantasy, something to long for, something to wish for, something to dream about. But there are a few among us who seem to have it all.

They have the three things that our world today

embraces and exalts and adores most of all. They have what modern-day advertising repeatedly tells us we must have in order to be happy. They have the big three: wealth, youth, and power.

Rod Wilmoth tells about just such a person. Her name was Renee. By the young age of twenty-five, Renee was already more successful than most people are in a lifetime. She was bringing in a big salary with a high-profile company, and she owned a staggering stream of highly valuable properties. She owned a gorgeous home, possessed an incredible wardrobe, and drove a fully equipped silver luxury sports car.

Bright, articulate, attractive, creative, ambitious, meticulous, deliberate, persuasive, perceptive—Renee was all of these and much, much more. She had an amazing ability for figuring out fine-print escrow clauses, and her talent was paying off handsomely for her. She had it all—wealth, youth, and power.

But, somehow, something was missing. There was a void, an emptiness, a sense of futility. Not long ago, Renee drove her silver sports car to the beach. There, she checked into a hotel and then checked out of life with an overdose of pills. Just twenty-five years young, she left behind a note that said she was ending her life. She just couldn't go on, because, she said, "I am so tired of clapping with one hand." Isn't that a haunting, poignant line? *I am so tired of clapping with one hand.*

It is so tragic to see how someone like Renee, who had it all—wealth and youth and power—could end up like that—tired and bored and empty and depressed.

She reminds me of the rich young ruler in Mark 10. (See also Matthew 19:16-30; Luke 18:18-30.) Here we discover a person who is truly blessed. He too has wealth and youth and power, but here in Mark 10, we find him coming to Jesus looking for life and meaning and fulfillment. Why? Because he is tired of clapping with one hand!

Here is a man who is rich materially. He is young in age. He is a big success. He's a leader, a ruler, a man with considerable clout and power. And yet, those things are not enough. Despite all he has, there is something lacking, something missing, a void, an emptiness, a hunger. There is no excitement in his life, no zest, no joy, no sense of purpose or mission. Rod Wilmoth puts it like this:

> He had his youth and wealth (and power), but his life had all the zing of a wet tennis ball. It was lifeless. It lacked bounce.
>
> Jesus saw immediately that the young man had been trying to "bliss out on wealth" so he told him to have a garage sale.
>
> Go, sell what you have and give it to the poor (and come follow me and you will find greater treasure) and you will find the other hand with which to clap.
>
> But, it was too drastic a remedy for the young man who had grown so accustomed to the security of his youth and wealth. So, he turned away sadly and lived out his life clapping with one hand (From a sermon given on Oct. 13, 1985).

What went wrong for that young man? Was it "too much, too soon"? Sometimes that is the perfect setup for heartache. Or had he been spoiled from the beginning? And was he now coming face-to-face with the fact that selfishness ultimately is boring and unfulfilling? Or maybe he suddenly realized that respectability is simply not enough.

Have you heard the story about the pastor and the astronomer who happened to sit next to each other on an airplane one day? They struck up a conversation.

The astronomer was something of a cynic about religion, and finally he said to the pastor, "You know, Reverend, I think you folks make way too much of religion. In fact, I think all religions can be summed up in a simple saying in just two words: Be respectable."

The pastor thought about the astronomer's comment for a moment, and then he said, "Well, in like manner, I'm fairly sure that all astronomy can pretty well be summed up in a simple saying as well as in just ten words: 'Twinkle, twinkle, little star, how I wonder what you are.' "

One of the things the story of the rich young man teaches us is that respectability is not enough, being a success is not enough. We have to look higher than this world for our happiness.

The rich young ruler was on the right track for a while that day. He realized that he was empty inside, and he came to the right place for help. He came to Jesus! He came to Jesus in search of real life. The only problem was, he didn't finish what he started; he didn't see it through; he didn't do what Jesus told him to do; he couldn't make the leap of faith; he turned away sorrowfully. Why? What held him back? Why didn't he follow Jesus? Let me suggest three reasons; and as we look at these things that held the rich young man back, we just might find ourselves somewhere between the lines.

First of All, He Was Not Able to Prioritize

He couldn't get his priorities straight. He was so wrapped up in his material possessions that he couldn't see that Jesus was offering him something better.

Jesus was not fussing at wealth that day. He was saying, "Hey! Look—following me is *better* than riches; it is the greatest treasure in the world. It is wealth beyond counting."

Rudyard Kipling spoke of this once. He said, "The world will tell you to be greatly concerned about money, position, or glory, but then someday you will meet a person who cares for none of these things. Then you will know how poor you are."

Sometimes we look at this story and emphasize the cost

of discipleship—in other words, what we have to give up to follow Christ. But if you look at this closely you will see that Jesus is not talking about the *cost* of discipleship here, but the *riches* of discipleship, and he is saying, "Discipleship is better than dollars! It's the top priority, the most important, the most worthwhile, the most valuable thing in the world."

Let me ask you something:

- Are you tired of going through life clapping with one hand?
- Do you want to be happy?
- Do you want to be excited about life?
- Do you want to be full of zest and excitement?
- Do you want your life to count for something?

If so, here's what you do:

- Accept Jesus Christ as your Savior, and commit your life to following and serving him.
- Commit your life to being his disciple.
- Commit your life to continuing his ministry of love.

Have you seen the movie *Field of Dreams?* In the movie a touching parable is told about life and death and reconciliation and forgiveness. The main character, played by Kevin Costner, is driven to find an old doctor, played by Burt Lancaster.

The doctor (many years before, as a young man) had been a professional baseball player. He had made it to the major leagues. But he had only gotten in the game for one play before his career ended. He didn't even get a chance to bat.

The rest of his life was spent as a small-town doctor whose love and caring were legendary. In the movie, the old doctor is offered a chance to return magically to his youth and to re-enter the big leagues to become the major league baseball star his talent had promised. It was a chance at fame and power and wealth. But the old doctor declined.

"But you only got to play five minutes in the big leagues," he is told. "That's a tragedy!"

"No," he replies. "If I had only gotten to be a doctor for five minutes, *that* would have been a tragedy." (Quote is from Clyde Fant in *Pulpit Digest*, Sept.-Oct. 1991; p. 38.)

The doctor had his priorities straight, didn't he?

Some years ago, Albert Schweitzer, speaking to a graduating class in an English school, said, "I do not know what your destiny will be. Some of you will perhaps occupy remarkable positions. But I do know one thing: The only ones among you who will be really happy are those who have sought and found how to serve Christ."

The rich young ruler's problem was that he had his priorities out of whack. He didn't understand what Jesus was offering him. He turned away from the greatest treasure in the world. Please don't let that happen to you.

If you want life, *real* life, if you want a sense of joy and purpose and mission, then come to Jesus Christ and accept his call to service and discipleship. Follow him and you will find the greatest treasure this world has ever known.

That's number one: The rich young ruler was not able to prioritize. And the question for us is, Can we?

Second, He Was Not Able to Love

The rich young man could not bring himself to reach out to the needy. He could not find it in his heart to love; and that's why he was going through life clapping with one hand.

As World War II was winding down and the outcome was certain, one prisoner of war camp decided to release half of their prisoners. The prisoners were told that at nine o'clock the next morning, a list of names would be posted, and those whose names were listed would be taken to a boat and given their freedom. Those who names were not on the list would remain in the prison camp. Those to be set free could take with them only one duffel bag.

In that camp were two soldiers who were close friends. They had been together throughout the war and throughout the horrible prison camp experience. They had helped each other, encouraged each other, looked out for each other.

Sadly, one of their names was on the list, the other was not. One was selected to be set free, the other would be forced to stay behind in prison.

The soldier to be set free went to gather his most prized personal belongings. He placed them in his duffel bag. But then, as he started toward the boat and toward his freedom, he saw his friend, and he realized that his friend had not been selected.

Quickly, the soldier motioned his buddy to follow him. Discreetly, they went behind one of the barracks. The soldier turned his duffel bag upside down and poured out all of his personal possessions onto the ground. He opened the duffel bag wide and told his friend to get into the bag. He then strenuously lifted the duffel bag onto his back and carried it onto the boat—and to freedom—the most important, the most precious, the most valuable thing in his life: his friend!

He was a smart and courageous soldier, wasn't he? Are you that smart? Am I? For, you see, only two things really matter in this world—our relationship to God, and our relationships with others. If you want to be happy, if you want to be full of life, then learn how to love! Live in the spirit of Christ. Let the love of God flow through you and out to others.

That's what Jesus was trying to teach the rich young ruler. Sadly, he missed the message. Please don't let that happen to you. The rich young ruler was not able to prioritize, and he was not able to love. The question for us today is, Can we?

Third, He Was Not Able to Trust

Jesus called him to discipleship, but the rich young ruler could not trust Jesus enough to make the leap of faith. He felt too secure where he was. His was a pampered and comfortable life. He was bored and unfulfilled, but he was secure; to walk away from that would take a high level of trust. Sadly, he couldn't do it. Sadly, he turned away. It takes a lot of trust to make the leap of faith.

I like the way Norman Vincent Peale put it several years ago in a funeral sermon for a friend. He said:

> Now, if a baby not yet born, still tucked under his mother's heart, could think, he might say to himself: "This is a wonderful place. It's warm. I'm fed. I'm taken care of. I'm secure. This is a great world where I am now. I like it here." And then someone might say to him: "But you're not going to stay here. You have to move on. You're going to die out of this place. You're going to another world." The baby would look upon the process of birth as if it were death since it would be the end of the pleasant state he was in. But look what happens to him! He is cradled in loving arms. Soft hands hold him gently. A kind face looks down at him and he loves that face. Everybody that comes near loves him. He's the king of the world he surveys and he comes to love that world, too. It's even better than the one in which he had been before.
>
> Finally, he gets to be an old man and he is told: "You have to die to this world." He protests: "I don't want to die. I love this world. I like the feel of the sun on my face and the cool rain. I love the faces of my wife and children. I've lived here a long time and I love this place. I don't want to die."
>
> But, he does die to this world and then he is born into the next. And look what happens! He awakens to find himself young again. And once again, there are loving faces to greet

him and loving hands to touch him. And even more beautiful, sunlight will be there to surround him, and sweeter music than he's ever heard in his life before will sound in his ears.

And all tears will be wiped from his eyes and he will say: "Why was I so afraid of this thing called death, when, as I now know it is really life instead?"

You know, if the rich young ruler had trusted Christ and followed him, if he had trusted Christ and if he had become his disciple, I know without question he would have later said, "Why was I so afraid of this thing called discipleship, when, as I now know, it is really life—exciting, fulfilling, meaningful life that enables us to clap with both hands!" It enables us to feel the rain and not just get wet.

9

Can You Feel the Quality of Childlikeness?

What Our Children Are Teaching Us

People were bringing little children to him in order that he might touch them; and the disciples spoke sternly to them. But when Jesus saw this, he was indignant and said to them, "Let the little children come to me; do not stop them; for it is to such as these that the kingdom of God belongs. Truly I tell you, whoever does not receive the kingdom of God as a little child will never enter it." And he took them up in his arms, laid his hands on them, and blessed them.

—Mark 10:13-16

Some years ago, Andrew Gillies wrote a poignant poem called "Two Prayers." The first prayer is the prayer of a little boy who kneels one evening at his bed, confesses some childish wrong, and then through tears asks God to help him to grow up to be a wise, strong, and good man like his dad.

The second prayer is spoken by the dad. As his little son sleeps peacefully, the father prays that God will make him childlike in his faith like his son who is so pure, genuine, trusting, and sincere.

I like that poem for a couple of reasons. For one thing, it reminds me personally of how much I have learned from my children. They are so special, and they have taught me so much over the years. But the poem also reminds me of the dramatic scene in Mark 10 where Jesus blesses the children and says, "Truly I tell you, whoever does not receive the kingdom of God [like] a little child will never enter it" (verse 15). How relevant those words are for us today, because we in our modern, urbane, "success-at-any-cost" world are so prone to become too tough-minded, too sophisticated, too cynical, too hard-hearted, too businesslike, too image-conscious, too cold and calculating.

Somehow in recent years, so many people in our world have become so jaded and so harsh and so critical of everyone and of everything. For example, a media frenzy was created a few years ago when basketball superstar Michael Jordan ended his "first" retirement from professional basketball and reentered the NBA. Why the frenzy? Because Jordan changed the number on his basketball jersey. Some news reporters went absolutely bananas. They bashed him mercilessly. Much ink was spilled over that one. But think about it. In the ultimate scheme of things, did it really matter whether Michael Jordan wore number 45 or number 23 on his Chicago Bulls jersey? Why do we build our heroes up and then take such delight in trying to tear them down?

An even more distressing sign of the times occurred a few years back when Mother Teresa (still living at that time) came under fire from some "critics." Can you believe it? This sweet, dedicated, hard-working, compassionate, committed eighty-four-year-old nun who was giving her life to helping people who are destitute and dying—and they were attacking her? There were complaints that Mother Teresa was using all of her energy to help needy individuals and therefore was not attacking the social ills of Calcutta. When I read of that, I couldn't help myself. I said out loud, "Give me a break!" Surely we have better things to do than to trash Mother Teresa.

Somehow over the years, so many people in our world

have become so heavy-handed, so angry, so suspicious, so derisive. They have lost the quality of childlikeness! They have become so caught up in their own self-importance that they think they have to constantly blow the whistle and sound the alarm and be the prophets of doom. They want to be the watchdogs of society—and, unfortunately, for too many, they have become attack dogs. They have lost the joy and wonder and innocence of childhood. You can see the problem written boldly in the worried, anguished look always present on their faces.

In a lighter but similar fashion, this is what the disciples were going through in Judea that day. Caught up in their own self-importance, they were "throwing their weight around," swaggering about, acting sophisticated, barking out their commands: "Get back there you kids! Get those children out of here! This is serious business! We don't have time for this! We are doing big things up here! Don't bother the Master! Get back and keep quiet! He doesn't have time for children!"

But when Jesus saw what they were doing, he was displeased. "No! No! No!" he said to them. "Don't do that! Let the children come to me! And remember this," he said. "Whoever does not receive the kingdom of God like a little child will never enter it."

Obviously, Jesus is referring here not to *childishness*, but to child*like*ness. He probably was drawing attention to the qualities of genuineness, receptivity, dependence, trust, love, openness, affection, curiosity, energy, enthusiasm, joy, and wonder. All of these are characteristic of children, and they are also characteristic of the true Christian lifestyle. Elton Trueblood said it well in *The Heart of a Child:*

We tend to glorify adulthood and wisdom and worldly prudence, but the Gospel reverses all that. The Gospel says that the inescapable condition of entrance into the divine fellowship is that we turn and become as a little child...tender and full of wonder and unspoiled by the hard skepticism on which we so often pride ourselves. God has sent children into the world, not only to replenish it, but to serve also as sacred reminders of something ineffably precious which we are always in danger of losing...[the quality of childlikeness]. Thus, the sacrament of childhood is [always for us] a continuing education.

With that in mind, let's think together for a few moments about the great lessons our children are teaching us. There are many, of course. Let me mention three of them. I'm sure you will think of others.

First, There Is Gratitude

Some years ago in a midwestern town, a little boy was born blind. His mother and father were heartsick, but they struggled with his blindness the best they could. Like all such parents, they prayed and hoped for some miracle. They wanted so much for their son to be able to see. Then one day, when the little boy was five years old, the community doctor told them that he had heard about a surgeon at Massachusetts General Hospital who was specializing in a new surgical procedure that might just work for their son, that might just give their little boy his eyesight.

The parents became excited at the prospect, but when they investigated further and discovered the cost of the surgery and the travel and the hospital expense involved, they became deflated because they were not people of great means. In fact, some would call them poor. But word got out in the community, and their church rallied to help them. In a short period of time, the money was raised to send them to Boston for the surgery. On the morning they were to leave for Boston, the little boy gathered his things together, including his tattered little teddy bear. It had an ear chewed off, was missing an eye, and was bursting at the seams. The boy's mother said, "Son, why don't you leave that old teddy bear at home? He's about worn out. Maybe we can buy you a new one in Boston or when we get back." But the boy said, "No, I need it."

So off to Boston they went. He held tightly to that teddy bear all the way. The surgeon sensed how important the teddy bear was to the little boy, so he allowed the boy to keep the bear with him throughout all the many examinations prior to surgery. On the morning of the surgery, the hospital staff brought in two surgical gowns, one for the little boy and a smaller version for the teddy bear, and off to the operating room they went—a little blind boy on a stretcher, holding on dearly to his beloved teddy bear.

The surgery went well. The doctor felt good about what they were able to accomplish. "I think he will be able to see," said the surgeon, "but we won't know for sure until we remove the bandages in a few days." Finally, the day came for the doctor to remove the bandages. The nurses and interns stood with the parents as the surgeon slowly unwound the gauze from the boy's eyes. Miracle of miracles! The little boy could see! For the first time in his life he saw his mother's face, he saw his father and his doctor, he saw flowers and candy and balloons, and the people who had cared for him. For the first time in his life, he saw his teddy bear. It was a joyous celebration!

When it came time for the boy to leave the hospital, his surgeon came into the room. The doctor had grown so attached to the little boy that he had to busy himself with those insignificant gestures that we do when we are trying to surmount a great wall of emotion. They said their goodbyes with tears of joy all around. And then the doctor turned to leave. The little boy called him back. "Doctor," the little boy said, "I want you to have this." He was holding out the teddy bear! The doctor tried to refuse, but the little boy insisted: "Doctor, I don't have any money. So, I want to give you my teddy bear to pay you for helping me to see. I want you to have it. It's my way of saying, 'Thanks.' "

The doctor took the teddy bear and shook the little boy's hand and wished him well. For a long time after that, on the tenth floor of the White Building of Massachusetts General Hospital, there was on display a teddy bear, bursting at the seams, with a chewed-off ear and one eye. And there was a sign under it written in the hand of that surgeon. It read, "This is the highest fee I have ever received for professional services rendered." (Thanks to Leonard Sweet, *Sweet's Soul Cafe*, Feb. 1995; p. 6.)

That little boy, so thrilled that he now could see, in response gave away his most prized possession. There's a name for that: It's called thanksgiving. Of course, that kind of appreciation has to be learned. But when our children learn it, and express it so beautifully, it touches us and teaches us—the beauty, the power, the importance, and the necessity of gratitude.

Second, There Is Love

It was a cold Christmas Eve a few years ago. Will Willimon, dean of the Chapel at Duke University, was rushing his family to get into the car. They were running late for the communion service. "Where are the sermon notes? Where is the pulpit robe? Don't forget to turn off the lights. Everybody get in the car and be quiet!" On the way to the church, rushing through the traffic, their five-year-old daughter, Harriet, got sick at her stomach and vomited all over the car. "Great!" Will Willimon thought, "If people only knew what preachers go through." He wheeled into the church parking lot and jumped out of the car, leaving his wife, Patsy, to clean up the car and get the kids into church. And he thought, "If people only knew what preachers' spouses go through."

Patsy led a still unsteady and pale Harriet into the church. They sat on the back pew in the darkness—just in case Harriet got sick again. Their son, William, age seven, ran down to the front of the church to sit with his grandparents. Will Willimon threw on his robe, took a deep breath, and joined the choir for the processional. He made it through the first part of the service, and the sermon. Then came Holy Communion. Will Willimon's wife, Patsy, came down to the altar to receive the sacrament, but she left Harriet on the back pew. Harriet was still so pale and so weak and sick.

But then something beautiful happened. Seven-year-old William got up and came back to the communion rail. "What on earth is he doing?" wondered his parents. "He's already received Communion once. What is he up to?" They watched him race to the back of the church and scoot down the pew toward his sister. He opened his hands, revealing a small piece of bread. "Harriet," he said, "this is the body of Christ, given for you."

Without hesitation, little Harriet picked the bread out of her brother's hands and plopped it into her mouth and said, "Amen." And in that moment, Holy Communion had never been more holy. William patted his sister on the head. She smiled. He smiled. And then he turned and ran back down to the front of the church to rejoin his grandparents (Thanks to William Willimon for the use of this story. See *The Christian Ministry*, July-Aug. 1989; p. 47). Think of that. No one else thought about Harriet. No one else thought to include her. No one else reached out to meet her need that night, except her seven-year-old brother, William.

There's a name for that. It's called love! What a beautiful thing it is when our children rise to the occasion and teach us once again the power of love, the wonder of love, the miracle of love.

Third and Finally, There Is Faith

What is faith? It's trusting God, come what may. It's committing your life to him and trusting him in every circumstance. My brother, Bob, who is a pastor in Memphis, recently shared with me a moving story that makes the point.

A little girl had somehow gotten a bad cut in the soft flesh of her eyelid. The doctor knew that some stitches were needed, but he also knew that because of the location of the cut he should not use an anesthetic. He talked with the little girl, and he told her what he must do. He asked her if she thought she could stand the touch of the needle without jumping. She thought for a moment and then said, simply, "I think I can, if Daddy will hold me while you do it."

So the father took his little girl in his lap, steadied her head against his shoulder, and held her tightly in his arms. The surgeon then quickly did his work, sewing up the cut in her eyelid, and the little girl did not flinch. She just held on tightly to her father. That's a parable for us in our spiritual lives, and a graphic reminder that whatever we have to face, we can hold on tight to our Father, and he will see us through.

There's a word for that. It's called trust, or faith. It's surely what Jesus had in mind when he said, "Unless you become like a little child, you cannot enter the kingdom of God." It's surely what Paul had in mind when he said, "I'm ready for anything, for Christ is my strength." The quality of faith, the commitment to trust in God, come what may; the spirit of childlikeness is so important, and our children have so much to teach us. How great it is when they teach us the powerful lessons of gratitude and love and faith!

10

Can You Feel the Firm Foundation?

Upon This Rock I Will Build My Church

Now when Jesus came into the district of Caesarea Philippi, he asked his disciples, "Who do people say that the Son of Man is?" And they said, "Some say John the Baptist, but others Elijah, and still others Jeremiah or one of the prophets." He said to them, "But who do you say that I am?" Simon Peter answered, "You are the Messiah, the Son of the living God." And Jesus answered him, "Blessed are you, Simon son of Jonah! For flesh and blood has not revealed this to you, but my Father in heaven. And I tell you, you are Peter, and on this rock I will build my church, and the gates of Hades will not prevail against it. I will give you the keys of the kingdom of heaven, and whatever you bind on earth will be bound in heaven, and whatever you loose on earth will be loosed in heaven." Then he sternly ordered the disciples not to tell anyone that he was the Messiah.

—Matthew 16:13-20

A group of birds got together one day and decided to establish a church. A meeting was called so that they might discuss the matter and decide what they wanted in their church—what was most important and what their church should be.

The parrot stood and said, "If we are going to have a church, we've got to have organization. We need committees, subcommittees, officers, and lots of them. Yes, no question about it: Organization is the single most important thing in the church today."

The pheasant jumped up and said, "I disagree. Organization is all right, but it's much more important to have lots of big social events. We all have beautiful feathers, and surely God meant for us to show them off. Yes, the most important thing in the church is lots of big, sparkling social events."

The sparrow chimed in. "No! It's a popular pastor. *That's* what we need the most. Doesn't matter what he says or does, so long as he doesn't ruffle anybody's feathers. Yes, a popular pastor; *that's* the most crucial thing."

The starling shouted out, "Well, I think you are all wrong! Most important of all is to have a beautiful building."

Next, the mockingbird spoke up: "We need a pastor who is good with young people. That's the key thing—to straighten out these wild young people and keep them off the streets."

Then the cardinal (who had just flown in from St. Louis) said, "Well, I think we need a baseball team. The most important thing of all is to have a good baseball team to represent our church. That is vital!"

Well, it was glaringly obvious that there was widespread disagreement as to what was most important in the church. But then, the wise old owl slowly rose to his feet, and all grew quiet as he prepared to speak (for he was noted for his great wisdom). In a reassuring manner, the wise old owl said, "Despair not, my friends, for we can have all these things."

The other birds obediently chimed in, "All these things! Yes, we can have all these things!" They congratulated one another, they shook hands, they patted one another on the back, and thus they formed their church. And when they got through, do you know what they had? That's right—they had a "church for the birds"! A "church for the birds" *not* because of what they had included, but because of what they had left out. A "church for the birds" because there was no good news, no message of God's grace— indeed, no regard for God at all. It was a "church for the birds" because there was no sense of mission or morality, no compassion for others, no thought of sharing the Savior's love, no understanding of service, and no commitment to Christ; no challenge toward Christlike living.

Now, of course we know that it helps to be organized, it's good to have social events, it's wonderful to have a capable staff and a beautiful facility. But these things become significant only when they spring forth from our commitment to Jesus Christ. These things become significant and sacred only when they enable us to do the work of Jesus Christ.

A few years ago at an annual conference, Bishop Ben Oliphint quoted noted jazz musician Fats Waller. Fats Waller's father was a minister, and Fats Waller (wanting to help his dad) would write gospel hymns to sing in church. One of his hymns had this line: "Everything that's not of Jesus will go down!" This is uniquely true of the church. If you build a church that's not of Jesus, that's not caught up in the spirit and mission of Jesus Christ, it will not last, it will not endure, it will go down!

That is precisely what this remarkable passage in Matthew 16 is all about. What a powerful scene this is. Jesus is nearly ready to head toward that showdown in Jerusalem. He decides to check out the progress of his disciples. Do they really understand what's happening? Do they really understand what awaits them in Jerusalem and beyond? Do they really understand who he is? Jesus stops and asks them, "Who do people say that I am?" They answer, "Well, some say you are John the Baptist and others say Elijah and others Jeremiah or one of the prophets."

Then Jesus asks them that powerful, personal question that has resounded across the ages: "But who do you say that I am?" Simon Peter (always the bold spokesman) says, "You are the Messiah [Christ], the Son of the living God." Jesus then says this: "Blessed are you, Simon son of Jonah! For flesh and blood has not revealed this to you, but my Father in heaven. And I tell you, you are Peter, and on this rock I will build my church."

What is going on here? What rock is Jesus talking about? What does this mean? It means that rock-solid commitment to Christ is the only sure foundation for any church! If you have that rock-solid commitment to Christ, your church can withstand any storm. If you don't have that, your church will not last. It will have no staying power. It will either be ripped apart by the hard storms of life without or it will crumble and fall apart because of decay within. Or, as Fats Waller put it in his gospel hymn, "Everything that's not of Jesus will go down."

Now, let me be more specific and try to bring this closer to home. There are three very special qualities that are always found in the firm foundation on which the church must be built.

First of All, There Is the Rock of Faith

Lou Holtz, former head coach of the Notre Dame Fighting Irish football team and now coach of the South Carolina Gamecocks, is a great motivational speaker. He is in demand all over the country. One of his favorite stories is about a man who accidentally ran his car into a ditch out in the country. The man was not hurt at all, but he was stuck and couldn't get out. He asked a farmer for help. The farmer said, "I have an old mule named Dusty. I think he can pull you out." The farmer hooked Dusty up to the car, and when all was ready, the farmer snapped the reins and shouted, "Pull, Jack! Pull, Joe! Pull, Tom! Pull, Dusty!"

Amazingly, that old mule pulled the car out of the ditch with relative ease. The car owner was impressed and grateful. He thanked the farmer profusely, and then he said to the farmer, "Let me ask you something. Why did you call Dusty by four different names?"

The farmer replied: "Well, you see, it's like this. Old Dusty's eyesight is just about gone, and if he thought for a minute that he were the only one pulling, he wouldn't have tried at all!"

The faith that holds the church together and keeps the church going is rooted in the good news that we are not alone! Unlike Dusty, we really have somebody helping us. Christ is with us. We can count on that. And we can count on him. He is our strength. He is our comforter. He is our salvation. We can face anything because he is with us. Remember how Jesus put it, "I am with you always, to the end of the age" (Matthew 28:20).

Let me tell you something: I am sold on the church! Do you know why? Because there is no institution in the world that serves people like the church. There is no institution in the world that helps families like the church. There is no institution in the world that redeems lives like the church. There is no institution in the world that teaches love like the church. There is no institution in the world that lifts God up like the church, and there is good reason for that. It's because there is no institution in the world that has Jesus Christ like the church.

The world is starving to death for Jesus Christ, and we as Christians have him. That's the bottom line. We are here as people of faith to share Jesus Christ with a needy world, and everything we do is for that purpose. We have worship services and Sunday school classes. We have prayer groups, support groups, Bible study groups, youth groups, children's groups, singles groups, senior adult groups, and mission work groups. We take trips, we put on dramas, we play games, we present concerts, we paint houses, we build clinics, we feed the hungry, we help the needy. And all for one purpose—so we can share the love and presence of Jesus Christ, so we can tell people about him.

Christ is with us. That's what is right with the church, and that is our sure foundation—our Rock of faith.

Second, There Is the Rock of Hope

Recently I visited a friend of mine in the hospital. She had been very sick and very weak for several days, but now she is on the road to recovering rapidly. She told me that the members of her Sunday school class had been angels to her—angels of love, angels of mercy, angels of encouragement, and angels of hope. "They wouldn't give up," she said gratefully. "They put life back into me."

Many of you know well the name of Jackie Robinson. He was one of the greatest baseball players of all time. He was the first African American to play in the major leagues. He broke the color barrier, and because of that he lived under incredible pressure. Bigotry screamed at him from every direction. Prejudicial insults came his way daily. Horrible obscenities were shouted at him constantly. He received all kinds of hate mail and all kinds of death threats.

One day he received a particularly disturbing telephone call with a violent threat, just before he took to the field. It unnerved him. That day, Jackie Robinson was so shaken by the pressure and the threats that he lost his focus, and for one of the few times in his life, he was having a bad game. He struck out with the bases loaded. Then shortly after, he made a fielding error at second base. The crowd began to boo him unmercifully.

Pee Wee Reese, his teammate, called time-out. He went over and put his arm around Jackie Robinson and said, "Jackie, let me tell you something. I believe in you. You are the greatest ballplayer I have ever seen. You can do it. I know that. And I know something else: One of these days you are going into the Hall of Fame. So, hold your head up high...and play ball like only you can do it." A few innings later, Jackie Robinson got the hit that won the game for his team, the Brooklyn Dodgers.

Some years later, when Jackie Robinson was indeed inducted into baseball's Hall of Fame, he remembered that moment: "Pee Wee Reese was my friend," he said. "He believed in me. He saved my life and my career that day. I had lost my confidence, and Pee Wee picked me up with his words of encouragement. He gave me hope when all hope was gone."

We in the church are called to be "angels of hope" to one another like that, yet even more so, because our hope is not built upon our ability. No, as the hymn writer Edward Mote put it, "My hope is built on nothing less than Jesus' blood and righteousness. On Christ the solid rock [we] stand, all other ground is sinking sand" ("My Hope Is Built," 1834). First, there is the Rock of faith, second, there is the Rock of hope.

Third and Finally, There Is the Rock of Love

Lee McKinzie, one of the ministers on the staff of the church I serve, was on sick leave a few years ago and was out for two months. On April 3, 1995 (a Monday afternoon), Lee had a heart catheterization performed on him. He had been experiencing some tightness in his chest. The "heart cath" went well, and the doctor was explaining to Lee that a couple of places had been found that needed attention, but that he was confident the problems could be corrected in a noninvasive way.

In typical fashion, Lee was joking with the doctor when suddenly things "turned south." Lee began to have double vision, then his words began to slur, and then he went into a coma. This is very rare, but somehow a blood clot had broken loose from somewhere and had hit the stem of the brain. Fortunately, the clot began to dissolve on its own.

The following evening (Tuesday night), Lee was still in a coma, and we wanted him to hurry and wake up. The doctors sensed our obvious concern and said to us the words we needed to hear: "We are expecting Lee to fully recover, and we want you to expect that. However, you must understand that when something like this happens, the coma may last one day, two days, three days, maybe even seven days. I know you want him to hurry and wake up and talk to you. We don't know precisely when that is going to happen, but he will come out of it. And he will recover."

The next morning (Wednesday morning), we had our staff meeting. I was explaining all of this to our staff and reminding them of the importance of our being patient. "We don't know how long Lee will be unconscious, but the doctors are optimistic, and they want us to be optimistic," I said. We then had a prayer and went on with our meeting. About ten minutes later, our volunteer receptionist walked into the room and handed me a note. All eyes were on that note. I stopped the meeting and read it out loud. "Lee is awake!"

One person started singing the Doxology, and all the staff joined in. And through our tears of joy and gratitude, we sang the Doxology like it had never been sung before. "Praise God from whom all blessings flow..." And I thought to myself, "This is what love is, and this is what the church is all about—faith, hope and love!" A church built on the Rock of Love in Christ cannot fail. It will—by the grace of God—endure and prevail to the end of time!

11

Can You Feel the Good Side of Worry?

Is It Wrong to Worry?

"Therefore I tell you, do not worry about your life, what you will eat or what you will drink, or about your body, what you will wear. Is not life more than food, and the body more than clothing? Look at the birds of the air; they neither sow nor reap nor gather into barns, and yet your heavenly Father feeds them. Are you not of more value than they? And can any of you by worrying add a single hour to your span of life? And why do you worry about clothing? Consider the lilies of the field, how they grow; they neither toil nor spin, yet I tell you, even Solomon in all his glory was not clothed like one of these. But if God so clothes the grass of the field, which is alive today and tomorrow is thrown into the oven, will he not much more clothe you—you of little faith? Therefore do not worry, saying, 'What will we eat?' or 'What will we drink?' or 'What will we wear?' For it is the Gentiles who strive for all these things; and indeed your heavenly Father knows that you need all these things. But strive first for the kingdom of God and his righteousness, and all these things will be given to you as well.

"So do not worry about tomorrow, for tomorrow will bring worries of its own. Today's trouble is enough for today."

—Matthew 6:25-34

A new pop song swept the country a decade ago. It soared to the top of music charts all over America. President George Bush was in the White House at the time, and he called it one of his personal favorites. The song had a catchy rhythm and a light fun sound. Do you remember it? It was called "Don't Worry, Be Happy!"

That little song captured such widespread interest that one major car company even tried to capitalize on its popularity by creating an expensive advertising campaign based on the theme "Don't Worry! Buy Honda!"

It's still true isn't it? Everywhere we go these days, we are bombarded with the message "Don't worry! Don't worry!" (Concerns about the Y2K problem and the millennium notwithstanding.) For example, go to the bookstore and you will find all kinds of new self-help books on this subject, books like

- *How to Stop Worrying and Start Living*
- *How to Kick the Worry Habit!*
- *Spiritual Vitamins for Worriers*
- *How to Trust More and Worry Less*
- *How to Cope When You're as Worried as a Long-Tailed Cat in a Room Full of Rocking Chairs!*

Or go to the drugstore, and you will discover all kinds of medicines designed to reduce tension, anxiety, and worry, numerous prescriptions and medical aids to calm us down, to settle our fears, to help us sleep, to ease our stress, and to relieve our apprehensions.

Even bumper stickers preach about this. I saw one the other day that said "Worry is like a rocking chair: It's something to do, but it won't get you anywhere!" Another read "Stop Stewing and Start Cooking!"

Now, the very fact that so much is being written or prescribed with regard to the problem of worry tells us something. It tells us that there is a big market out there for these books and medicines and bumper stickers; that there are lots of folks out there these days who feel plagued with the agony of worry; that there are large numbers of chronic worriers in our world today who are screaming for help and looking for answers. It tells us that we who live in this stressful world not only worry, but we worry that we are *worrying* too much! Now, hold on to your seats because I want to tell you something that I think is tremendously important about this. You may soon forget much of what you are reading right now, but I hope you will long remember this. Are you ready? Here it is: Even though it is said to us over and over, "Don't worry! Don't worry!" the truth is that we cannot stop worrying! **We cannot stop worrying because God has put within us (for our own good) a certain amount of worry energy or anxiety energy. We all have worry energy naturally within us. It is part of our basic makeup and it's there for good reason.**

So, the question is not, Will we worry? We *will!* We can count on that! The question is, How do we use our worry energy creatively? How do we use our worry energy productively?

The question is, Are we directing our worry energy toward the real priorities of life?

The question is, Are we letting our worry energy motivate us and pull us up into positive action rather than deplete us and push us down into self-pity?

The problem is not that we worry, it's that many of us do not know how to worry meaningfully or how to put our worries to work or how to use this anxiety energy for good! If we never worried about our children, we would be terrible parents. If we had no concern for our nation or our city, we would be awful citizens. If we never worried about our jobs or had no consideration for a job well done, we would be pitiful workers. If we had absolutely no concern for our church, we would be pathetic church members. If we never worried about making ends meet, we would be in big trouble!

So the key is to learn how to worry *creatively.* Jesus

gives us some great lessons about that in Matthew 6. Here is lesson number one.

First, to Worry Creatively Means to Let Our Worries Work for Us Rather Than Against Us

Now, let me hurry to emphasize that there is a huge difference between creative worry and silly fretting. Creative worry spurs us into action. Silly fretting paralyzes us, handcuffs us, imprisons us, disables us. Creative worry works for us. Silly fretting works against us.

In the Sermon on the Mount in Matthew 6, when Jesus tells us, "Do not be anxious" (RSV), he is not talking about creative worry. He is not talking about thoughtful consideration, or loving concern, or careful, sensible planning. Rather, he is talking about silly, useless, immature fretting. The Greek word used here for "anxious" is a fascinating and revealing one. It is *merimnao,* a combination of two smaller words—*merge,* which means to divide, and, *nous,* which means the mind. In other words, Jesus is saying, "Beware the divided mind. Don't get your priorities mixed up."

There is a poem called "The Worry Cow." In the poem, the cow would have kept on living, but she lost her breath because:

> She thought her hay wouldn't last all day,
> So she mooed herself to death.

That kind of worry can kill. It robs us of our vitality and poise and the ability to think straight. It makes emotional wrecks of us, takes away the radiance of living, and makes us mere skeletons of our real selves.

The noted writer Thomas Carlyle once built a sound-proof room in his home in London so he could do his work without interference from outside noises. The reason he did this was because his neighbor had a rooster that crowed, and the crowing bothered Carlyle. Carlyle protested to the neighbor, but the neighbor answered that his rooster crowed only three times a day, and surely that was not a great annoyance. "But," Carlyle said to him, "If you only knew what I suffer just waiting for that rooster to crow!"

Many of us can relate to that, can't we? We wait and worry, just knowing that something terrible is going to happen to us at any moment. We wait and wait, and worry and worry, and thus our energies are washed out and our strength depleted.

But take a close look at the things that fret you. Do they really happen? *Do* they? *The Boston Transcript* used to carry these words at the top of its front page: "I am an old man. I have worried a great deal about many things, most of which never happened."

Another writer, John Watson, in *The Houston Post,* put it like this some years ago: "What does your anxiety do? It does not empty tomorrow of its sorrow; it only empties today of its strength. It does not make you escape trouble; it only makes you unfit to cope with it when it comes."

This kind of silly, useless, immature fretting is what Jesus is warning us about here in Matthew 6 when he says, "Do not be anxious." But, there is another kind of concern, another kind of worry that is actually productive—the worry that spurs us to action, the concern that motivates us to do something creative and productive. For example, if I never worried, I would never write a sermon. To get it done, to get it completed, to get it right and to get it finished, I have to get anxious about it. That worry energy, that anxiety energy, that concern prompts me, stirs me, moves me to get with the program and to get done what needs to be done.

One popular athletic-shoe television commercial made the point. It encouraged us to get in shape with the theme

"Just do it." That's the bottom line: "Just do it!" The point is, we can stew and fret about needing to exercise more, or we can just do it.

So, first, creative worry means to let our worries work for us rather than against us, to let our worries move us to action. Now, here is the second point.

To Worry Creatively Means to Let Our Worries Be Directed Toward Matters That Really Matter

Let me ask you something. What are you worried about right now?

—A dent in the car? A health problem?

—The economy? Your vacation? The weather?

—Your next hair appointment? A party invitation?

—A problem at work? The homeless?

—The hungry? The kingdom of God?

—Your marriage? Your children? Your favorite sports team?

—What to name your new cat? Where to have lunch?

—Or how long the Sunday sermon is going to last?

You see, our worry list says a lot about us—and about our priorities. What we are anxious about *right now* reveals a lot about what is really important to us. Jesus preached his greatest sermon to the world's great worriers. The people who heard him that day when he preached the Sermon on the Mount were people who worried themselves silly over countless washings, keeping minute laws, fasts, feasts, and traditions. And they were also fretful over social status and taxes and money and death. Really, their list of worries was not so different from ours.

And Jesus said to them and to us, "Don't be so anxious! Don't be so nervous! Don't be so fretful!"

He also gave us a magnificent solution. He said, "Strive first for God's kingdom and his righteousness, and everything else will fall into place for you. Just make God the King of your life; work at that, set your mind on that, and God will bring it out right. Do the best you can each day, and then turn it over to God" (Matthew 6:33 paraphrased).

Do you remember going to the circus as a child? They had chameleons that could change their colors to match their environment. Put them on a brown coat, and they would turn brown; put them on a green coat, and they would turn green. Well, Carl Sandburg once told of a chameleon who made it just fine changing his colors to match his environment until one day he accidentally crawled onto a scotch-plaid sportcoat. He had a nervous breakdown heroically trying to relate to everything at once!

Some of our worries are simply the consequence of forgetting our priorities. To worry creatively means, first, to let our worries work for us rather than against us, and second, to let our worries be directed toward matters that really matter.

Third and Finally, to Worry Creatively Means to Let Our Worries Bring Us Back to God

Abraham Lincoln expressed it this way: "I have been driven many times to my knees by the overwhelming conviction that I had nowhere else to go."

Some years ago, a young man named George Matheson entered Glasgow University. He had a keen mind. His hopes were high. Soon he and his fiancée would be married. He dreamed of a bright future. But then the bottom dropped out. He lost his eyesight.

Then, because of his misfortune, Matheson was rejected by his fiancée (who said she couldn't marry a man who was blind and left him). His world crumbled at his feet. Devastated, afraid, worried, he turned to God as never before, and God was there!

Struck blind, hurt, rejected, George Matheson reached out in the darkness and found that God's love is always there for us. And he wrote what has become one of our most beloved hymns, a hymn sung by Christians everywhere that says it all, a hymn of praise to God:

> O Love that wilt not let me go,
>   I rest my weary soul in thee;
> I give thee back the life I owe,
>   that in thine ocean depths its flow,
>   may richer, fuller be.

("O Love That Wilt Not Let Me Go," 1882)

That is the answer to the problem of worry. It's the "blessed assurance" that no matter what difficulties we have to face, God will always be there for us, and he will see us through. We can claim that promise, and we can live in that confidence!

12

Can You Feel the New
Way of Looking at Things?

Are You Looking the Wrong Way?

As Pharaoh drew near, the Israelites looked back, and there were the Egyptians advancing on them. In great fear the Israelites cried out to the LORD. They said to Moses, "Was it because there were no graves in Egypt that you have taken us away to die in the wilderness? What have you done to us, bringing us out of Egypt? Is this not the very thing we told you in Egypt, 'Let us alone and let us serve the Egyptians'? For it would have been better for us to serve the Egyptians than to die in the wilderness." But Moses said to the people, "Do not be afraid, stand firm, and see the deliverance that the LORD will accomplish for you today; for the Egyptians whom you see today you shall never see again. The LORD will fight for you, and you have only to keep still."

Then the LORD said to Moses, "Why do you cry out to me? Tell the Israelites to go forward."

—Exodus 14:10-15

Mark Twain once described the day he rushed to the top of Pike's Peak to see the sun rise. He said, "I got there on time, but I missed it because I was looking the wrong way!" This is a common problem in life, isn't it? God has so many fantastic sunrises to show us, so many dramatic miracles to share with us, so many awesome wonders to reveal to us—but all too often we miss them because we are facing the wrong direction.

117

We have eyes, but so often we do not see; we have ears, but so often we do not hear; we have hearts, but so often we do not feel, because we are looking the wrong way, facing the wrong direction. Remember that powerful passage in the book of Exodus where Moses experiences the presence of God in the burning bush? (Exod. 3). Moses is so moved by the sacredness of that moment that he "takes off his shoes" as an act of reverence, because he knows that he stands on holy ground.

Reflecting on the burning bush episode, Elizabeth Barrett Browning wrote these words:

> Earth's crammed with heaven
> And every common bush afire with God.
> And only he who sees takes off his shoes,
> The rest sit around and pluck blackberries.

The *way* we see is so important, so crucial. Harold Kushner, in his book *Who Needs God?* expresses it this way:

> Religion is not primarily a set of beliefs, a collection of prayers, or a series of rituals. Religion is first and foremost a way of seeing. It can't change the facts about the world we live in, but it can change the way we see those facts, and that in itself can...make a real difference. (N.Y.: Summit Books, 1989; p. 27)

That is precisely what the remarkable story in Exodus 14 is about. It's about how people see things—how *differently* people may see the same situation.

On the one hand, look at what the people of Israel see here. They have just made camp at the Red Sea. They are filled with joy. This is an historic moment for them. This is their exodus, their deliverance, their salvation. After all those years of being slaves to the Egyptians, they are now free. Moses is leading them out of bondage to freedom in the promised land.

But suddenly, their beautiful dream becomes a ghastly nightmare. They turn around to look back, and on the horizon, far off in the distance, they see a huge cloud of dust, and they hear the unmistakable rumble of chariots. They know what this means. Pharaoh has changed his mind. His army is coming after them! The people of Israel see themselves as doomed and "done in." They see themselves trapped, pinned in, cornered, caught between the Pharaoh and the deep Red Sea. They are certain that they are going to be slaughtered in the desert. They see their situation as hopeless. You know why, don't you? Because they are looking the wrong way.

But on the other hand, Moses sees it so differently. He turns his face toward God and sees an exciting, amazing, incredible new possibility. Notice that Moses doesn't look to the past; he looks to the future! He doesn't look backward; he looks forward! He doesn't look at the strength of Pharaoh; he looks to the power of God! And because of what he sees, Moses is able to say to the people, with confidence, "Do not be afraid, stand firm, and see the deliverance that the LORD will accomplish for you today.... The LORD will fight for you" (Exod. 14:13-14). And then God says to Moses, "Tell the Israelites to go forward" (verse 15).

You know the rest of the story. Moses and the people of Israel do indeed put their trust in God and go forward. God goes before them, and he opens the sea, leading them to safety and freedom on the other side. God comes to the people in their hour of need. God saves them, protects them, delivers them. And he can do that for you and me. That's the good news of the Bible and the strong message that explodes out of this story.

But this story also confronts us with a crucial question, namely this: Are we looking the wrong way? Are we facing the wrong direction? Do we look at things with the eyes of fear or of faith? with the scared eyes of the Israelites or with the confident eyes of Moses? Let me break this down just a bit with three observations.

First of All, If We Can't See How to Believe, We May Be Looking the Wrong Way

This was the Israelites' problem that day at the Red Sea. They couldn't believe because they were looking the wrong way. They could see no hope because they were facing the wrong direction. God had to turn them around before they could see any way out of their predicament. That's the way it works. Before we can believe, the eyes of fear have to give way to the eyes of faith. We often hear the phrase "seeing is believing," but actually it may well be more profoundly true the other way around—believing is seeing!

This is precisely what happened to Francis of Assisi, and that change of vision is what made him a saint. He was awakened to a new way of looking at things, and that made all the difference. Francis was born into luxury. He was the son of a wealthy merchant. Early on, he had his eyes set on becoming a famous poet and a mighty warrior. He wanted fame and acclaim and power for himself. But during one of the military campaigns for his city-state, Francis of Assisi became ill, and he had to limp home in disgrace.

His adolescent vision of grandeur was reduced to shambles, and he went into a deep depression. He was so depressed that he retreated into a cave and remained there alone for almost two weeks. But, there in that cave, Francis was not really alone. God was with him, and God opened his eyes. God turned his life around. God saved him, delivered him, and gave him a new way of looking at things. Francis of Assisi came out of that cave a new man, and he went on to become one of the greatest servant-Christians in the history of the world. The name of St. Francis is now synonymous with love and humility and service and self-giving.

G. K. Chesterton, in his biography of St. Francis, describes the conversion of St. Francis in an interesting way. Chesterton said that Francis came "out of the cave 'walking on his hands.' " He now saw everything from a different perspective. When you are on your feet, "castles and trees seem to sit solidly on their own, as if they existed in their own right." But, when you stand on your head, "the same things appear literally to be 'hanging,' the way a chandelier hangs by its chain" (John Claypool, *Opening Blind Eyes*, Abingdon Press, 1983; p. 108).

Chesterton said that what Francis of Assisi discovered "is that everything 'hangs,' or depends, on God. This was the secret of St. Francis's incredible power to affirm and love everything he encountered. The birds, the animals, the trees, the flowers, people from every station in life, all spoke to him of God. Why? Because his eyes had been turned from self to God, from arrogance to humility, from greed to grace, from egotism, to service. Now, Francis of Assisi felt kinship with every particle of creation because his eyes had been opened to the fact that "all is miracle because all is of God" (Claypool, 108).

Back in the early 1960s, we were involved in the space race with Russia. They would send up a cosmonaut, and we would send up an astronaut. One of the Russian cosmonauts returned from his flight into outer space and somewhat arrogantly announced to the world that he "didn't see God up there anywhere." John Glenn was asked about this, and he said, "I saw God everywhere I looked!"

We can see God everywhere we look if we have converted eyes, if we see with the eyes of faith. If we can't see how to believe, we may be looking the wrong way.

Second, If We Can't See How to Forgive, We May Be Looking the Wrong Way

It's fascinating to watch how people act when trouble comes into their lives. You can tell a lot about a person by the way he or she handles a troublesome situation. Sadly, all too often we think the first thing we have to do when trouble comes is to find somebody to blame it on, and we can be so harsh, so unbending, and so unforgiving when we see it from that perspective.

That is precisely what the people of Israel did that day at the Red Sea. When they saw Pharaoh's army coming after them, they went into a panic, and they were quick to mouth and murmur, quick to gripe and complain, and quick to point the finger at Moses. "It's all your fault, Moses! Look what you have done to us! You should have left us alone! Our blood is on your hands! We will never forgive you for getting us into this mess!" You know why they reacted like that, don't you? Because they were looking the wrong way.

A few years ago, my friend Don Shelby was conducting a funeral service. He noticed a woman standing at the back of the sanctuary. The woman had arrived late and stood, hugging the rear wall and crying throughout the service. When the service ended, she came forward and in anguish hugged the casket. She broke down, sobbing and shouting into the casket, "I forgive you, Suzie! I forgive you! Can you hear me? Please hear me! I'm so sorry for the way I've acted. I love you. I forgive you. Please forgive me! Please forgive me!"

Don Shelby went to her and put his arm around her shoulders and held her, trying to comfort her. He could feel her pain. She looked up at him through her tears and she said, "My sister, Suzie, and I had a falling out some time ago. She begged me to forgive her. She tried everything to reconcile us. But over all these years I refused. I was so mean to her. I wanted her to pay for what she did to me. But I see now how wrong I was. I only wish to God I had listened to her. I loved her so much, and deep down I wanted things to be right with us. But now it's too late! I waited too long!"

Let me ask you something: Are you estranged from anyone like that today? Are you? Are you at odds with anybody? Are you cut off from someone? Are you holding a grudge? Are you suffering the spiritual gangrene of a broken relationship? If so, *go fix it!* Go be reconciled! Go clear it up today! For their sake, for your sake, for God's sake— go make peace!

Broken relationships are too painful, too stressful, too debilitating. They bring ulcers and headaches and insomnia and loneliness. What a way to live; it's *no* way to live! Go fix it. Go in the spirit of Christ. Go in the spirit of forgiveness and be a peacemaker. But, you may say, "It's not my fault!" Well, it may *not* be your *fault,* but as a Christian, it is your *responsibility.* Jesus underscored that over and over again. (See Matthew 18:21-22.)

The teachings of Jesus make it abundantly clear that nothing pleases God more than to see us actively and tenderly loving one another and caring for one another. And nothing breaks God's heart more quickly than to see us being harsh and cold and hateful toward one another. If we can't see how to forgive, we are facing the wrong direction, we are looking the wrong way.

Third and Finally, If We Can't See How to Trust, We May Be Looking the Wrong Way

That day when the Israelites felt trapped at the Red Sea, they lost their confidence. They were so blinded by the threat of Pharaoh's army that they failed to take into account the awesome power of God. Moses had to turn them around because they were facing the wrong direction. Moses had to remind them that God was with them, that God would fight for them, that God would deliver them. Moses had to remind them to trust God and go forward. That's a message we need to hear, isn't it? Sometimes we simply have to trust God and go forward, and know with confidence that he will see us through and bring it out right.

Do you remember that scene from *The Sound of Music* where Maria is being sent out from the abbey to be the governess for Captain von Trapp's seven children? She's a little nervous as she walks down the road, but to rally her courage, she begins to sing, "I Have Confidence. Let them bring on all their problems. I'll do better than the best. I have confidence they'll put me to the test, but I'll make them see I have confidence in me." But, just then she arrives and sees the huge, elegant, vast von Trapp estate, and she becomes intimidated, frightened, discombobulated. She stops singing, looks pleadingly toward heaven, and says prayerfully to God, "Oh, help!"

We can all relate to that, can't we? Sometimes life's problems simply overwhelm us, and all we can do is look to God and say, "O God, help me!"

The good news is that we can always count on God to be there for us and to give us the strength we need. We can trust him. Over the years, I have noticed something interested regarding this. I have come to see that God will give us the strength we need to face whatever problems confront us; but God, very wisely, does not give us that strength in advance because he knows that if he does, we may think the power comes from us and not from him.

Helen H. Lemmel phrased it beautifully in her hymn:

> Turn your eyes upon Jesus,
> Look full in his wonderful face,
> And the things of earth
> Will grow strangely dim
> In the light of his glory and grace.

("Turn Your Eyes Upon Jesus," 1922)

13

Can You Feel the Miracle of Encouragement?

Encourage Means to "Put the Heart In"

Now the eleven disciples went to Galilee, to the mountain to which Jesus had directed them. When they saw him, they worshiped him; but some doubted. And Jesus came and said to them, "All authority in heaven and on earth has been given to me. Go therefore and make disciples of all nations, baptizing them in the name of the Father and of the Son and of the Holy Spirit, and teaching them to obey everything that I have commanded you. And remember, I am with you always, to the end of the age."

—Matthew 28:16-20

Baseball fans will quickly recognize the name Brett Butler. Brett Butler was a highly respected major league baseball player. He played center field for the Atlanta Braves, the Los Angeles Dodgers, and the New York Mets. Butler was considered by many to be one of the finest lead-off hitters in the history of professional baseball. He was at one time recognized far and wide as the best bunter in baseball. He stole more than forty bases a year and usually scored more than a hundred runs each year.

In 1990, Brett Butler led the National League with 160 singles and 288 times on base. He made the Major League All-Star team in 1991 and was in the top ten in hitting in 1992. And he has done all of this despite being one of the smallest players in the major leagues. Brett Butler is only

125

5 feet 9 inches tall, weighs only 156 pounds, and wears size 7 shoes (the tiniest shoes in all of baseball). Coaches, teammates, opposing players, sports writers, and baseball fans everywhere had great appreciation for Brett Butler.

But that had not always been the case. Brett Butler did not have a fun youth. He was a tiny kid in junior high, so tiny that the rest of the guys in school picked on him and taunted him and laughed at him. "Every day for two years," Brett says, "the other kids in junior high would chase me around the playground. I would run and run and finally just run home. Every day for two years."

For Brett Butler, the perils of being small didn't end at age twelve. When he played football in high school, they had to go to the junior high school to get his pads because he was so small. He played quarterback and had to roll out just to see over the offensive line. His voice was so high-pitched that it cracked when he tried to bark out the signals, and the players on the other team would laugh at him and mock him. When Brett Butler told his high school coaches he wanted to play baseball in college, even they laughed at him and discouraged him. But Brett grabbed his glove and went off to college anyway—and eventually he became a two-time All-American.

When Brett again expressed an interest in playing professional baseball, people around him scoffed and laughed and teased him about being so small. But in 1979, the Atlanta Braves drafted him—in the 23rd round, which meant his chances of making it were slim to none. Nevertheless, Brett Butler overcame the odds and went on to win the job of starting center fielder for the Los Angeles Dodgers.

Did Brett Butler make it to the major leagues on the basis of pure athletic ability? Of course not. Here is the secret truth that we need to tell every young person in this land. The very best are those who work harder and who never quit. It's true in sports, in business, in music, in every endeavor in life. The secret of life is passion, determination, desire, perseverance, commitment. But in addition to all those good things, Brett Butler had something else working for him that is very special. At every point, at every obstacle, at every level, at every hard, discouraging moment, Brett Butler had a mother and father standing with him and for him and saying, "Brett, we are with you. We believe in you. We really believe in you. We know you can do it no matter what happens, no matter what anybody else says, we believe in you!" (Adapted from the article "A Good Thing in a Small Package" by Greg Johnson in *Youth Magazine*, May 1993; pp. 27-28.)

There's a name for that. It's called love! But it's also called the "miracle of encouragement." In French, the word *encourage* literally means "to put the heart in," while to *discourage* is "to tear the heart out." Over the years, with all those obstacles and challenges, with all those taunts and put-downs Brett Butler had to endure, I'm sure that his mother and father had to put the heart back into him many, many times. We all need that, don't we? The miracle of encouragement.

This is precisely what the passage in Matthew 28 is all about. Jesus is putting the heart back into the disciples. He is performing the miracle of encouragement. They are scared, confused, anxious, unsure of themselves, and the risen Lord is saying to them, I believe in you. I've got an important job for you. I'm counting on you. I know you can do this. Go spread the gospel across the face of the earth. Go teach the faith. Go make disciples of all nations. Go be a light to the world. Go, and I will go with you."

The miracle of encouragement is so important, so vital, so crucial. When the church and the home and the school are at their best, this is the message they join their voices to say to their children of all ages: "We love you! We prize you! We believe in you! We need you to take the good news of Jesus Christ out into all the world. We know you can do it, and we know that if you will open your heart to him, God will go with you. God will be there for you!"

I want so much for us to imitate the encouraging spirit of the risen Christ that we see so dramatically in this powerful passage at the end of Matthew 28. In a way, this was a graduation exercise for the disciples. Jesus had been teaching them, training them, preparing them, and now he is sending them out into the world. They are a little scared. Jesus senses the fear of the disciples. He knows about their anxiety and their uncertainty, so he comes to them—and look at what he does! He puts the heart back into them. He performs the miracle of encouragement.

It is so important that we take up that torch to follow his lead and to work constantly at performing the miracle of encouragement, to look constantly for ways to lift people up and put the heart back into them. We in the church are called to be people of encouragement. Let me be more specific with three thoughts.

First, We Are Called to Be People of Encouragement in Our Families

We get enough discouragement out there in the world. Our homes and our families should be instruments of encouragement.

In anticipation of Mother's Day a few years ago, Ellen Shepard (who was our children's minister at the time) and other members of our family life council did a series of interviews with some of our church members. They visited with people of all ages (from two to ninety-two) and asked them to reflect on their mother's love. We compiled their responses and handed out copies to people as they arrived at church. Let me share a few of these with you, because they underscore the point, the power of encouragement in our families.

One person said, "I see my mother as a positive force,

urging me forward, yet always behind me if I should fall."

Another said, "Mom wipes away the tears and celebrates the joys."

Still another said, "My mother was my friend when no one else was my friend. She is the example of unconditional love."

Yet another said, "My mom is cool because she didn't get mad when I blew up my fish tank and sixteen gallons of water soaked my carpet."

One other said, "My mother was always there for the small events and the big events. And sometimes being there for the small events meant even more."

There's a name for that. It's called love. But it's also called the miracle of encouragement.

There is a wonderful poem entitled "If I Had My Child to Raise Over Again." The poem was written by a wise mother named Diane Loomans. Ms. Loomans and her daughter, Julia, are the coauthors of the book *Full Esteem Ahead*. Listen to these powerful words:

> If I had my child to raise all over again...
> I'd finger paint more and point the finger less.
> I'd do less correcting and more connecting.
> I'd take my eyes off my watch and watch with my eyes.
> I would care to know less and know to care more.
> I'd take more hikes and fly more kites.
> I'd stop playing serious and seriously play.
> I'd run through more fields and gaze at more stars.
> I'd do more hugging and less tugging.
> I would be firm less often and affirm much more.
> I'd build self-esteem first, and the house later.
> I'd teach less about the love of power,
> And more about the power of love.

(Thanks to my administrative assistant, Cynthia Sarver, for bringing this poem to my attention.)

Sometimes I am asked to do parenting workshops, and most always at a certain point I notice the same poignant reaction. I tell the parents that as parents, we must wear two hats at the same time—the "referee hat" and the "cheerleader hat." The referee hat reminds us that we must set rules and parameters. The cheerleader hat reminds us to cheer our children on, to say to them enthusiastically and often, "I love you. I believe in you. I'm so proud of you. I think you are terrific!"

Then I say to those parents, "I want you to think back over the last two weeks. Recall the words you have spoken to your children. How many of those words were 'referee' words? And how many were 'cheerleader' words?"

Here's where the poignant reaction happens. All across the room heads will drop, heads will bow, eyes will stare at the floor, because suddenly they realize that they have been doing lots of refereeing and not nearly enough cheering. As Christian people, our calling is to be people of encouragement in our families. That's number one.

Second, We Are Called to Be People of Encouragement in Our Churches

One of my favorite New Testament personalities is Barnabas. I like him because he lived out the meaning of his name. The name *Barnabas* literally means the "son of encouragement." That is precisely what Barnabas was—an encourager. We, in the church, are called to be present-day Barnabases, the sons and daughters of encouragement.

Some of you may be familiar with the name Jim Stockdale. Vice Admiral James B. Stockdale was a hero in the Vietnam War. He survived 2,714 days as a prisoner of war and was a powerful symbol of courage and strength for his fellow prisoners. On one occasion, the prison guards handcuffed Stockdale's hands behind his back, locked his legs in heavy irons, dragged him from his dark prison cell, and chained him to a post in a sunbaked courtyard, so that the other prisoners could see what happened to anybody who did not "toe the line" and cooperate. He was beaten and kicked repeatedly. He was not permitted to sleep. Every time he closed his eyes or nodded off, they would beat him again. This went on for three days and nights.

Jim Stockdale survived that horrendous ordeal. He lived to tell of it. And he said the thing that kept him going was one of the sweetest sounds he had ever heard. After every beating, he would hear the sound of snapping towels. His fellow prisoners would snap their towels. It was not random snapping. His fellow prisoners were snapping out a Morse code message: "G-B-U-J-S." Jim Stockdale knew what that meant. "G-B-U-J-S . . . God Bless You, Jim Stockdale!" That snapping of towels, that Morse code message of encouragement, gave Admiral Stockdale the strength he needed to survive that agonizing, debilitating, dehumanizing experience (Dr. Julius Segal, *Winning Life's Toughest Battles*, McGraw Hill, 1986).

That true story out of the Vietnam War is a pretty good parable for us, a good illustration of the church's role in caring for one another. Our calling as a church is to be there for people in the Spirit of Christ, in their joys and sorrows from the cradle to the grave; to be there for people in their pain, saying, "God bless you!" to be there performing the miracle of encouragement. My prayer is that we will be people of encouragement, in our families and in our churches.

Third, We Are Called to Be People of Encouragement in Our Faith

That's what Matthew 28 is really all about. In the last paragraph in Matthew's Gospel, we find some of the greatest words of encouragement in all of the Bible. The risen Lord promises to always be with us. No matter what, come what may, he will be with us! If that doesn't give us a sense of strength and confidence, I don't know what would.

David Letterman made it popular—the Top Ten List. However, the truth is that Top Ten Lists have been with us for a long, long time. The first and best Top Ten List is recorded in the book of Exodus. It's called The Ten Commandments. I have written a Top Ten List for us to remember as we make our faith journey out into all the world. Here they are:

10. *Remember that* it's best not to travel alone.

9. *Remember that* a sense of humor is not excess baggage.

8. *Remember that* the Bible is your best road map and your best instruction manual.

7. *Remember that* prayer means friendship with God and that friendship works best when the friends keep in touch.

6. *Remember that* no matter what obstacle may confront you, with the help of God you can rise above it.

5. *Remember to* stop and smell the roses.

4. *Remember that* as you encounter the detours and hard knocks of life, you have a choice: You can get bitter, or you can get better!

3. *Remember as you travel* to love unconditionally, to forgive unreservedly, and to serve unselfishly.

2. *Remember to* keep your battery charged by staying plugged into the Power Source.

1. *Remember to* be careful as you travel, because you are of great value—you *must* be—because Christ came and lived and died and rose again for you.

What Jesus said to his disciples long ago, he is saying to us today: "Go out into all the world and be my church. Be a light to the world. Proclaim the good news and perform the miracle of encouragement. Go and I will be with you always."

14

Can You Feel the Sense of What's Valuable?

Be Careful What You Throw Away

But we appeal to you, brothers and sisters, to respect those who labor among you, and have charge of you in the Lord and admonish you; esteem them very highly in love because of their work. Be at peace among yourselves. And we urge you, beloved to admonish the idlers, encourage the fainthearted, help the weak, be patient with all of them. See that none of you repays evil for evil, but always seek to do good to one another and to all. Rejoice always, pray without ceasing, give thanks in all circumstances; for this is the will of God in Christ Jesus for you. Do not quench the Spirit. Do not despise the words of prophets, but test everything; hold fast to what is good; abstain from every form of evil.

—1 Thessalonians 5:12-22

Some years ago, a talented young professional golfer joined the pro tour. He quickly captured the attention of the golf world with his unique ability. He showed tremendous promise. Since he was just starting out, he had no money, so some friends got together and raised money to send him to play in the Australian Open, and they made arrangements for him to stay with an Australian rancher.

The young golfer arrived early, and the rancher was showing him around his old home place. When they came to the barn, the young golfer noticed some old golf clubs stuck over in a back corner of the barn. They were obviously discarded, thrown away, because they had dust and cobwebs all over them. As golfers will do, the young pro pulled out one of the clubs. It happened to be the putter. He took a few practice strokes. "I like the feel of this putter," he said. The rancher answered, "Keep it! It's yours! My gift to you, although its not much of a gift. That old putter has seen its day, I'm afraid. It's pretty worthless, if you ask me. But, if you want it, it's yours!"

The young golfer thanked him, went back to his room, and stuck the old, discarded putter into his golf bag and forgot about it. The next day, the Australian Open golf tournament began. On the first green, the young golfer stood over his first putt of the day. He studied the difficult putt carefully and then reached back for his putter. Accidentally, his caddy handed him the old discarded putter. The young golfer prepared to putt. But then he realized he had the wrong putter in his hands.

He went on and used it anyway. And he made the putt! He kept on using that old discarded putter, and he kept on making his putts. And he won the Australian Open! Then he won the British Open. And over the years, he won many, many tournaments and became one of the greatest golfers the world has ever known, using an old discarded putter! By the way, the golfer's name was Bobby Jones. He named that old putter "Calamity Jane"!

The point is clear: Be careful what you discard. Be careful what you toss aside. Be careful what you label worthless. Be very careful what you throw away. This is what the apostle Paul is underscoring in his letter to the Thessalonians. In essence, he sums up that significant letter with these words: "Love one another. Rejoice always and pray constantly. Give thanks in all circumstances. Test everything, and hold fast to what is good." Hold on to what is good with both hands!

I don't know about you, but at the beginning of each year, I find myself wanting to clean and straighten. I want to clean out my closets and clean off my desk. I want to throw away a bunch of stuff that is cluttering up my life. I want to travel light. That's a good thing to do every now and then—to sort through and to throw away things we don't need anymore.

Recently, however, as I was going through this annual ritual of throwing stuff out, I thought of golfer Bobby Jones. I thought of how effectively and productively he had used that old, discarded putter—which someone else had branded absolutely worthless and had discarded—and I remembered the lesson in that example: Be very careful what you discard. Be very careful what you toss aside. Be very careful what you throw away. Or, as the apostle Paul put it, "Hold fast to what is good." Paul, of course, was not talking about physical things like tattered sweatshirts, or moth-eaten bathrobes, or out-of-style neckties, or worn-out sneakers, or antiquated putters. No, he was certainly talking about spiritual things when he said to "hold fast to what is good"; he was referring to things of the heart, the spirit, the soul. And he was sounding a word of caution: Be careful. Don't let the world confuse you about what the priorities are. Don't let the world perplex you about what is worthy and what is worthless. Don't let the world baffle you or bewitch you or mislead you. Test everything by the measuring stick of Christ's sacrificial love. And hold fast to what is good!

In 1 Thessalonians 5, Paul brings this point close to home for us as he describes three things that we need to hold on to with all our strength and power and might, three things we dare not discard. Here they are.

First of All, Don't Throw Away the Spirit of Gratitude

Hold on tight to the spirit of gratitude. Paul put it like this: "Give thanks in all circumstances" (1 Thessalonians 5:18a). Let me point out that Paul didn't say to give thanks *for* all circumstances. Obviously, we don't give thanks for cancer or heart attacks or arthritis or accidents. But we can give thanks *in* all circumstances because God is with us, come what may. And when we realize that and embrace that and reach out to God in faith, he will give us strength and see us through. We can count on that. And that is cause, indeed, for great thanksgiving.

Some years ago when I was in seminary, I went to theology class one morning, and Dr. David Shipley did something that day that was so dramatic it has stuck with me over all these years. We filed into the classroom, and Dr. Shipley stood at the front of the class in silence. When everybody was settled and totally quiet, he humbly prayed a brief but powerful prayer. Then, without saying a word, he walked to the chalkboard and drew a picture of the cross. Underneath, he wrote two words: *God's love.*

Without saying a word, Dr. Shipley then moved way over to the left of the cross and drew a series of arrows that moved toward the cross. Under this line of arrows moving toward the cross, he wrote these words: *In order to.* Then, Dr. Shipley moved to the other side of the cross, and starting at the cross, he made another series of arrows moving this time away from the cross. Underneath this line of arrows, he wrote these words: *Because of.* Then he stood there in silence for a long time, looking intently at what he had drawn on the board.

Finally, he turned toward the class and said to us in his polite style, "Ladies and gentlemen, do you have an 'In order to' faith or a 'Because of' faith?" No one answered. No one moved a muscle. The truth was, we didn't know what in the world he was talking about. He realized this and he said, "Let me help you. The arrows represent good works. The cross represents God's love. So the question is, Do you do good works in order to win God's love or because you already have God's love?"

Dr. Shipley then walked back to the board and crossed

out the "In order to" side, and he said, "Ladies and gentlemen, we don't have to win God's love. We already have it. It is freely given, graciously given! He showed us that on a cross, a long time ago. We have only to accept it in faith and then pass it on to others."

Then Dr. Shipley moved quickly over to the "Because of" side of the board, and he said, "Here's where we need to be, ladies and gentlemen. Here's where we need to be. We love God because he has first loved us. We serve God not 'in order to' woo him or win him or wow him, but 'because of' his gracious love already given to us through Jesus Christ, our Lord and Savior. We serve God out of gratitude for what he has already done for us on that cross! All Christian good works are expressions of gratitude. Thanks-giving is, simply put, Thanks-*living*; living out our thanks to God daily—*that* is the essential spirit of a Christian. Ladies and gentlemen, gratitude is so important."

That's why Paul said it long ago, and that's why I'm trying to say it now. "Hold fast to what is good." No matter what the world says to you, don't throw away the spirit of gratitude.

There is an old legend that tells about a man who came one day to the barn where Satan stores the seeds that he scatters across the earth. The man noticed that the two most abundant seeds in the barn were the seeds of bitterness and discouragement. He asked Satan about those seeds. "Oh yes," came the reply, "bitterness and discouragement; these are, without question, my most effective seeds. Why, these seeds will grow almost anywhere." Then, with a solemn look on his face, Satan said, "However, there is one place where the seeds of bitterness and discouragement will not grow."

"Oh?" said the man. "And where is that?"

Satan answered: "They will not grow in a heart of gratitude!"

Whatever you do, don't throw away the spirit of gratitude.

Second, Don't Throw Away the Spirit of Hope

Hold on tight to the spirit of hope. Paul expressed it like
this: "Rejoice always, and pray constantly." In other
words, no matter what problems or difficulties or troubles
or heartaches come your way, don't lose heart! Hang in
there. Stay positive. Trust God. And don't discard the spirit of hope.

A few years ago, a NFL team had high hopes of going to
the Super Bowl. They made the play-offs easily. However,
in their first play-off game, they played a terrible first half,
and as the second quarter wound down they found themselves behind, 21 to 0. The team members trudged to the
locker room. They were down and dejected, and they knew
what was coming. The coach was going to scream his lungs
out at them, and with good reason. They had played so
poorly, missed tackles, messed up blocking assignments,
dropped passes, run the wrong routes, flubbed kicks, committed numerous fumbles—you name it. They did it all
wrong, and they knew the head coach would let them have
it at halftime.

But, strangely, the coach didn't come into the locker
room. So the players just sat there in silence. No one said
a word. Instead, each one replayed in his mind how badly
he had done. Then, just before time to begin the second
half, the coach walked in. All he said to the team was one
simple thing, but somehow it got through to them, and
they went out and won the game. What did the coach say?
Just this: "Gentlemen, you've got a great second half inside
of you!"

When you stop to think about it, that is precisely what
God is saying to us every day: "You've got a great second half
inside of you." If you feel that you have stumbled or failed

or disappointed someone or fallen short of your best effort, or if you feel down and out and defeated, then listen carefully. God has a great word of hope for you. If you listen very closely, you can hear him. He is saying, "You've got a great second half inside of you! I believe in you! I will help you! I will give you the strength you need! I will stand with you!"

Whatever this world may say to you or do to you, don't ever believe that there is no hope. Where God is, there is help and there is hope. So whatever you do, don't throw away the spirit of gratitude, and don't throw away the spirit of hope.

Third, Don't Throw Away the Spirit of Love

Hold on to love with all of your strength. Paul said it this way: "Love one another. Do good to one another." The world will tell you that love is weak and that real strength is found in military might, political clout, and material things. But don't you believe that for a minute! Love is now, always has been, and always will be the most powerful thing in the world!

In my office, I have six huge volumes of Will Durant's study of history. He calls it *The Story of Civilization* (New York: Simon and Schuster, 1935).

Volume I is called *Our Oriental Heritage.* It has over 1,000 pages.
Volume II is called *The Life of Greece.* It has close to 800 pages.
Volume III is called *Caesar and Christ.* It has some 750 pages.
Volume IV is called *The Age of Faith.* Over 1,100 pages.
Volume V is on *The Renaissance.* About 750 pages.
Volume VI is on *The Reformation.* Over 1,000 pages.

Will Durant wrote five more volumes in this series, and numerous other volumes of history and philosophy. The point is, Dr. Will Durant was one of the most respected historians of this century. Someone asked him once: "Dr. Durant, you have written great volumes of history in your lifetime. What has history taught you?" Wisely, Will Durant answered, "I can sum it all up in three words— 2000 years of history in three words—love one another. My final lesson of history is the same as that of Jesus. Love one another. The world may try to tell you something different but you just try it. Love is the most powerful and most practical thing in the world" (Pam Procter, "The Ages of Love," *Parade*, August 6, 1978).

So be very careful what you discard. Don't throw away gratitude. Don't throw away hope. And don't throw away love. Hold fast to what is good. Hold fast to these good things.

15

Can You Feel the Beauty of Inclusiveness?

Breaking Down the Dividing Walls of Hostility

But now in Christ Jesus you who once were far off have been brought near by the blood of Christ. For he is our peace; in his flesh he has made both groups into one and has broken down the dividing wall, that is, the hostility between us. He has abolished the law with its commandments and ordinances, that he might create in himself one new humanity in place of the two, thus making peace, and might reconcile both groups to God in one body through the cross, thus putting to death that hostility through it. So he came and proclaimed peace to you who were far off and peace to those who were near; for through him both of us have access in one Spirit to the Father. So then you are no longer strangers and aliens, but you are citizens with the saints and also members of the household of God, built upon the foundation of the apostles and prophets, with Christ Jesus himself as the cornerstone. In him the whole structure is joined together and grows into a holy temple in the Lord; in whom you also are built together spiritually into a dwelling place for God.

—Ephesians 2:13-22

Bob Hayes tells a wonderful story about a young man who was an all-American football player in college. He went on to play professional football for a few years and then came back to his alma mater as an assistant coach. One of his main responsibilities in his new job would be to scout and recruit players for his college team. Before he made his first recruiting trip, he went in to visit with the head coach, the same coach for whom he had played when he was there in college some years before.

The head coach was a crusty old veteran. He had been the head coach for many years, and he was widely known and highly respected all across the country. The new young coach said to him, "Coach, I'm about to head out on my first recruiting trip, but before I go, I want to be sure that we are on the same page. Tell me, coach, what kind of player do you want me to recruit?"

The old head coach leaned back in his chair. He looked the young coach straight in the eye and said, "Son, I've been at this job a long time, and over the years I have noticed that there are several different kinds of players. For example, you will find some players who get knocked down and they stay down. That's not the kind we want." He also said, "You will find some players who get knocked down, and they will get right back up, and get knocked down again, and then they stay down. That's not the kind we want." And then, the old coach said, "But you will also find some other players who get knocked down and knocked down and knocked down, and every time they get knocked down, they get right back up!"

At this point, the young coach got excited, and he said: "Now, that's the kind of player we want, isn't it, coach?"

"No," said the old head coach, "we want the one doing all that knocking down!"

That's what we need on our church team—players who will do some knocking down; players who will knock down walls; players who will knock down walls of hostility; players who will knock down not other people, but rather walls that separate, estrange, and divide. We in the church are called to knock down walls of hate and hostility and to build bridges of love and reconciliation. That is what this powerful passage in Ephesians 2 is all about. It is one of the greatest statements in all of the Bible. Listen to this: "[Christ Jesus] is our peace; in his flesh he has made both groups into one and has broken down the dividing wall . . . the hostility between us. . . . So then [we] are no longer strangers and aliens, but [we] are . . . members of the household of God, . . . with Christ Jesus himself as the cornerstone" (Ephesians 2:14-20.)

There is a gospel song/hymn that has these words: "Jesus, Jesus, Jesus! There's just something about that name!" Indeed, there is. The name *Jesus*, of course, means "Savior" or "the Lord's helper," but it is also the Greek form of the Hebrew name *Joshua*. And we remember, of course, who Joshua was. He was the one who caused the walls to come tumbling down! Remember how the spiritual goes: "Joshua fit the battle of Jericho . . . and the walls come a-tumblin' down." So Jesus is well named, because he also is a wall breaker. He breaks down the dividing walls of hostility.

This passage in Ephesians 2 can be better understood when we see it against the backdrop of the physical make-up of the Temple in the time of Jesus. The Temple was a parable in stone, exposing the prejudices and the walls that existed in society during Bible times—walls that included a few privileged people but excluded and shut out most. As you moved through the Temple toward the High Altar (the Holy of Holies), there was a series of walls designed to hold people back from God.

1. The first wall held back foreigners, people of other races and nations. They could come inside the Temple, but only to this first wall.

2. The second wall held back the women and children. They could come into the Temple only so far; they could not come beyond this second wall.

3. The third wall held back Jewish men. They could come in farther than the foreigners and farther than the women, but not as far as the priests.

4. The fourth wall was a veil that surrounded the Holy of Holies, the High Altar, holding all back from God except the priests.

5. The High Priest was the only person who was permitted to go inside the veil, and he went in only once a year, on the Day of Atonement. And when he went inside the veil to the High Altar, a rope was tied around his ankle so that if he fainted or passed out or died while inside the veil, he could be pulled back out. The Holy of Holies, which represented the presence of God, was remote, fearsome, austere, and unapproachable.

But then came Jesus; and he broke down the dividing walls and made us one. He broke out from behind the walls, out from behind the veil, out to where the people were. That's what the Christian faith is all about—God breaking out, God smashing down the walls, God coming warmly and wonderfully into our lives.

Unfortunately, sometimes we forget that, and sadly, we start building up again those dividing walls, those walls that exclude and belittle and separate, those walls that encourage hostility and hatred and bigotry, walls that divide people, walls that divide nations, walls that divide races, walls that divide men and women, walls that divide families and neighbors, walls that divide and separate us from God.

Do you remember what happened in the Temple when Jesus was on the cross? The veil around the Holy of Holies, that veil around the High Altar, was torn apart from the top to the bottom. This was just another way of saying, "God did it! God tore that veil! God knocked down that wall!" That is the good news of our Christian faith. Christ is the Peacemaker, the Prince of Peace, the Reconciler, the Savior, the Healer. He makes us one. He breaks down the dividing walls of hostility and shows us that in him we are family. We are God's family.

But let me be more specific. Let me underscore some dangerous walls of hostility that plague and separate and divide people today. If we want to be Christ's servants, if we want to take up his torch, if we hope to continue his ministry and live in his spirit, then our calling is to join him in doing battle against these present-day walls of hostility that are so dangerous, so destructive, so divisive. Here's number one.

First, There Is Pride—Arrogant, Self-righteous Pride

Now, of course, we all know that there is a good kind of pride. It's great to be proud of your country and proud of your state and proud of your city and proud of your church and proud of your family and proud of your children and especially proud of your grandchildren. But that's not the kind of pride I'm talking about. I'm talking about that brand of pride that is arrogant and selfish and unbending. I mean that brand of pride that is the opposite of humility, the opposite of compassion. That kind of pride is destructive and divisive. Let me show you what I mean.

One evening, some years ago, a minister friend of mine visited a couple in their home. They had expressed some interest in joining the church, but my friend sensed an uneasiness; he could feel the tension and the stress in that home. Suddenly, the woman turned to her husband and said, "I'm going to tell him the truth. I'm going to tell him about our family." She went on: "This is killing me! It's eating me up! For seven years my husband and my son have not spoken to each other, although they have lived in the same house."

She pointed down the hall: "Look at that hallway. It's an average-size hall, yet they pass each other in it, brush against each other, and never speak." The mother said the son wanted to speak to his father and tried to, but the father ignored him. Finally, the teenager gave up. My minister friend turned to the man and asked him what had started the estrangement in the first place. Amazingly, the man admitted that the whole thing was so trivial that he really couldn't remember what it was! Yet, he said firmly, "I'm a proud man. I'm a man of my word. I vowed that I would never speak to that boy again, and I'm going to keep my word!"

Isn't that sad? Isn't that pathetic? Isn't that pitiful? What do you think Jesus would say to that man? I think he would say, "Come on now! That's enough! Knock down that wall of pride that's separating you from your son. It's not worth it. Go love your son! Go make peace with your son! Go reconcile! Go fix that! Get that divisive, destructive wall of pride out of there!"

Listen! Is your pride separating you from anybody today? Is your pride a dividing wall of hostility? Are you alienated from anybody? And, by the way, do you feel estranged from God? Is your pride keeping you away from God? If so, give it up! Let it go! If you will swallow your pride and turn to God in humility, God can make it right. God can bring peace to your troubled soul. God can fix those broken relationships; *if* you will swallow your pride.

Second, There Is Prejudice

Talk about a dividing wall of hostility; what can be worse than prejudice? The word *prejudice* means literally to prejudge, to judge without all the facts, to judge without really knowing the other person. And it is so wrong, so hurtful, so dangerous, so destructive. Any time we "look down our noses" at people who are different from us, any time we label other people or stereotype other people or ridicule other people or make jokes about other people or reject other people who are different from us, then we are building dividing walls of hostility. And it is so wrong.

Before Disney's musical production of *Beauty and the Beast* went to Broadway, it played here in Houston, where I live. We went down to the music hall to see it, and as we watched I realized that the story is a powerful parable about the danger of prejudice. Do you remember how the handsome prince was put under the spell that turned him into a beast? He was in front of his castle one day when what appeared to be an old beggar woman came by. She offered him a rose if he would give her shelter from the cold. But the prince was spoiled and selfish and arrogant, and he didn't want to have anything to do with the woman. He considered her to be "beneath" him, so he sneered at her and turned her away.

The woman said to him, "Prince, do not be deceived by appearances, for real beauty is within." But again, the prince sneered at her and rejected her and turned her away. Then the old beggar woman's ugliness melted away to reveal a beautiful enchantress. The prince apologized, but it was too late. She had seen no kindness or compassion in him. She had seen no love in his heart, so she cast a spell upon him that ruined his life, that devastated all of his relationships and made him a lonely and wretched beast! The only way he could be released from the spell would be to learn how to love and be loved. And that is precisely what happened. The young woman named Beauty came to his castle, and she saw beyond the Beast's outward appearance! She loved him and taught him how to love. And when *that* happened, the spell was lifted and he was redeemed! He was converted by love.

The point is clear: When we live under the spell of prejudice, we become something much less than what God meant us to be, and we need to be redeemed and converted by the beautiful, sacrificial love of Christ. Christ breaks down the dividing walls of pride and the dividing walls of prejudice.

Third and Finally, There Is Vengeance

Vengeance—the angry, bitter spirit that will not forgive, that nurses its wrath to keep it warm, that broods and festers and looks for a chance to get 'em back—what a dividing wall of hostility *that* is!

Recently, I saw a sign in a business that read "To err is human, to forgive is not our policy." Some people live by that policy, and it is so sad. Vengeance is a dividing wall and a spiritual poison. Think about it like this. If you put a plastic covering over a plant, the rain and sun can't get to it, and the plant will wither and wilt and ultimately die. Vengeance is like that plastic covering. We can't be spiritually healthy until that plastic covering is removed.

Let me ask you something. Has someone hurt you? Do you feel estranged or alienated or crossways with anybody? Do you have bitterness in your heart toward any other person? If so, go fix it! Don't wait around anymore. Don't put it off any longer. For your sake, for their sake, for God's sake—*go fix it!* Ask God to go with you; and with his help, go set it right, go break down that dividing wall of hostility.

Harry Emerson Fosdick once said that "Christianity is like beautiful music. It doesn't require defense or explanation. It requires rendition." If we want to serve Christ, if we want to do his work, if we want to live in his spirit, then our calling is to join forces with him in knocking down the dividing walls of pride and prejudice and vengeance and in building bridges of love, understanding, forgiveness, and inclusiveness.

Epilogue

Can You Feel God Hugging You to Life?

At that time Jesus said, "I thank you, Father, Lord of heaven and earth, because you have hidden these things from the wise and the intelligent and have revealed them to infants; yes, Father, for such was your gracious will. All things have been handed over to me by my Father; and no one knows the Son except the Father, and no one knows the Father except the Son and anyone to whom the Son chooses to reveal him.

"Come to me, all you that are weary and are carrying heavy burdens, and I will give you rest. Take my yoke upon you, and learn from me; for I am gentle and humble in heart, and you will find rest for your souls. For my yoke is easy, and my burden is light."

—Matthew 11:25-30

Let me begin with three illustrations. See if you can find the common thread that runs through them.

First, Dr. Leslie Weatherhead reminds us of that old legend about the flute of Moses, the flute that Moses played when he was a shepherd on the hillsides of Midian. After Moses' death, the flute became a treasured relic. It was a simple, primitive shepherd's flute, but some thought that it was just not ornate enough. After all, it was the flute of Moses! It should be very beautiful, they reasoned.

So they commissioned artists and workmen to make it more elaborate and attractive. They did so by overlaying the flute with gold and jewels and exquisite decorations. When they finished, it was very beautiful and elegant, but there was only one thing wrong: Now the flute could not make a sound! The flute could no longer be played.

Somehow the extensive decorations had robbed the flute of its simple, clear note and had ruined it as a musical

149

instrument. Its original purpose had been distorted. It looked good outwardly, but it couldn't play a note. Weatherhead went on to point out that sometimes we are guilty of doing that to the message of Jesus, that sometimes we so overlay it with creeds and ceremonies, with doctrines and verbiage, that we miss the basic message of our Lord.

The second illustration comes from a *Peanuts* comic strip. Lucy and her brother Linus are getting ready to go to church for the big Christmas program, when this conversation takes place:

LUCY: Linus, are you sure you know your piece for the Christmas program?
LINUS: I know it backwards and forwards and sideways and upside down! I could say it in my sleep!
LUCY: Yeah, well, I remember last year, how you forgot and how you almost goofed the whole program.
LINUS: Well, this is THIS year, and THIS year, I won't forget. Listen to this: And the angel said unto them, "Fear Not—for behold, I bring you good tidings of great joy which shall be to all people... "
LUCY: Say, that's pretty good.
LINUS: I *told* you I know it. I've got it nailed this year. I now have a memory like the proverbial elephant! Well, I'm going ahead to the church. I'll see you there.

The next picture depicts Linus walking along the sidewalk in the snow, rehearsing his part again: " 'For behold, I bring you good tidings of great joy which shall be to all people... ' Perfect. What a memory I have!"

The next frame shows Linus coming back in the front door of his home. Lucy says, "Linus? What in the world? I thought you just left!"

Linus answers, "I did, but I came back. I forgot where the church is" (Charles Shultz, *You Don't Look 35 Charlie Brown* [N.Y.: Holt, Rhinehart, Winston, 1985]).

Here is illustration number three. Dr. Wernher von Braun, the brilliant scientist who was so influential in the launching of the American space program, had a fascinating hobby in which he used his great skills in mathematics. Dr. von Braun enjoyed playing around in his head with six-digit numbers. That is, he liked to add, subtract, multiply, and divide six-digit numbers in his head. For example, he might take the number 993,741 and multiply it by 632,785, and without the help of a calculator, without paper and pencil, he could, within a matter of seconds, come up with the correct answer.

Once, when Dr. von Braun was on a train going to an important meeting in New York, he became intensely involved during the long ride with his hobby of working with six-digit numbers in his head. He became so engrossed in his game that midway there, he had to get off the train and make a long-distance call back home to ask his office where he was going and what he was supposed to do when he got there. He had gotten so involved in the complexities of the numbers game that he literally forgot his destination and the purpose of his mission!

These three illustrations show us that we can get so caught up in the hectic busywork of life that we actually forget to live; that we can become so preoccupied with the complexities of our day-to-day existence that we miss the true meaning of life; that we can even get so involved with the trappings and mechanics of religion that we may lose sight of our real purpose and drown out the basic message of our Lord.

We get on the train, but we forget where we are going! We memorize our part, but we forget where the church is! We overlay our faith with so much pomp and circumstance and showy stuff that we lose the music! Of course, we also have to be aware of the fact that we can make a mistake at the *other* end of the pole, the other extreme of *oversimplifying* the faith. There is the danger of that. But, now, recognizing that risk, I want to try to express the gospel in three simple words—the words of Jesus: "COME... WAIT...GO." That is the gospel in three basic words: COME, WAIT, GO.

COME—the call to life.

WAIT—the call to worship.

GO—the call to service.

Let's look together at these one at a time and see if we can hear the Master's unique call to each one of us somewhere between the lines.

Our Lord's First Word to Us Is "Come"

"Come to me, all you that are weary and are carrying heavy burdens, and I will give you rest...for your [troubled] souls" (Matthew 11:28-29). Let me ask you something. Be honest now: Do you have a troubled soul? Are you tired and weary? Do you feel lonely, burdened, rejected? Is there something missing in your life? If so, the Master has a special word for you. The word is "Come— Come to me."

Some years ago, a young man named Joseph Scriven was deeply in love with a beautiful young woman. They were so happy together. They were engaged to be married and were planning their wedding. But then, tragedy struck. A terrible boating accident occurred, and Joseph Scriven's fianceé was killed, snatched away from him so suddenly, so tragically. He was heartbroken, despondent, bitter, even suicidal. But then one day, out of the blue, he remembered something that turned it around for him. He remembered these words of Jesus: "Come unto me, and I will give you rest."

So, Joseph took his heavy heart to Christ, and he found there a deep and abiding consolation. He found there power and grace. He found there new life. And out of that experience, Joseph Scriven wrote some poignant words that now make up the text of one of the most beloved hymns of all time.

> What a friend we have in Jesus,
> All our sins and griefs to bear!
> What a privilege to carry
> Everything to God in prayer!
>
> Can we find a friend so faithful
> Who will all our sorrows share?
> Jesus knows our every weakness;
> Take it to the Lord in prayer.

("What a Friend We Have in Jesus," 1855)

Many of you will recognize the name of Lewis Grizzard. He was one of America's most popular writers, with his down-home style of humor. In his very folksy way, he often shared in his books and in his syndicated column some of his personal experiences while growing up in the state of Georgia. Once, he remembered something that happened at church when he was a teenager that had touched him and had stuck in his mind over all these years. He said:

> Church was about all we had [in my hometown of Moreland, Georgia]. Sunday school was at ten, but preaching was only twice a month. We shared sermons and the preacher with another flock down the road.
> What did they call it on Sunday night? MYF? [Once] we had a couple of rowdy brothers in town who broke into a store. They were juvenile first offenders. [They got caught, and] their punishment was to attend Methodist Youth Fellowship [every Sunday evening] for six months. The first night they were there, they beat up two fifth-graders and threw a Cokesbury hymnal at the lady who met with us and always brought cookies.
> She ducked in time and then looked them squarely in

their devilish eyes. Soft as the angel she was, she said, "I don't approve of what you boys did here tonight, and neither does Jesus. But if He can forgive you, I guess I'll have to."

[And then,] she handed them a plate of cookies, and last I heard both are daddies with steady jobs and rarely miss a Sunday [at church]. That was the first miracle I ever saw. (Lewis Grizzard, *Kathy Sue Loudermilk I Love You*, Peachtree Publishers, 1979; p. 6)

Call it a miracle. Call it grace. Call it love. Call it forgiveness, conversion, redemption, or new birth. Whatever we call it, it's what happens when people come to the Master. That's his first word to us. "COME! Come to me I will give you new life!"

Our Lord's Second Word to Us Is "Wait"

Several times in the Gospels, Jesus tells the disciples to wait. Wait here and pray. Wait here and watch. Wait here until I return. However, my favorite example is found in Luke's Gospel. It's after the Resurrection, and Jesus is promising them the gift of the Holy Spirit. He says these words: "Wait here until you are clothed with power from on high" (Luke 24:49 adapted). It's the call to worship. In worship, we are clothed with power from on high.

The famous statue of Christ by the noted artist Thorvaldsen is presently on display in a church in Copenhagen. Some years ago, a man took his teenage son there to see this magnificent work of art, but the boy was not impressed. He was obviously disappointed as he walked by the statue. His father sensed his mood and said to him, "Son, what's wrong?"

The son said, "I don't know what the artist was thinking about when he did this, because you can't even see the statue's face."

The father only smiled and said, "Let me show you something. Move closer. Kneel down and then look up."

The boy did that. He moved closer to the statue. He knelt down, and then he looked up—into the face of Christ! You see, we have to get on our knees to see the face of Christ.

That's precisely what worship is, isn't it? It's moving closer to our Lord. It's kneeling down before him. It's looking up into his face. We can't do that on the run. We can't do that in a rush. It's so important to slow down every now and then and let our souls catch up with our bodies.

I recently read a story that touched me. It was about a man who had gotten so caught up in the hectic pace of our time that he had become almost like a zombie. He was just going through the motions, working long, hard hours and then coming home tired, weary, depressed, and irritable. There was no zest, no fun, no laughter, no joy left in him. His family noticed it, of course, but they didn't know what to do. He would come home and just sit, sullenly and silently, and only occasionally would he speak—and then, to snap at them.

One night, the man was reading the newspaper on the couch in the den, using the paper to wall out the rest of the family. Suddenly, his four-year-old daughter pushed the paper down, jumped into his lap, put her little arms around his neck, and hugged him tightly. With some exasperation, the father said to her, "Wait a minute, honey. You are hugging me to death!"

"Oh, no, Daddy," she cried, "I'm hugging you to life!"

That's what God does for us in worship. He hugs us to life! Jesus knew how much we all need that, and that's why he said, "Wait. Wait here and worship, and you will be clothed with power from on high." First, Jesus says, "Come." And second, he says, "Wait."

Our Lord's Third Word to Us Is "Go"

Come, Wait, Go.

Come to life—Wait and worship—Then go to serve!

In 1970, Malcolm Muggeridge went to Calcutta to do a special documentary on Mother Teresa for BBC television. It was early one morning that he found her, working out in the streets with sick and poor people in a ghetto like he had never seen before, amid stench, filth, garbage, disease, and poverty that was just unbelievable. But what struck Muggeridge more than anything else, even there in that awful squalor and decadence, was the deep, warm glow on Mother Teresa's face and the deep, warm love in her eyes.

"Do you do this every day?" he asked.

"Oh, yes," she replied, "it is my mission. It is how I serve and love my Lord."

"How long have you been doing this? How many months?"

"Months?" said Mother Teresa. "Not months, but years. Maybe eighteen years."

"Eighteen years!" exclaimed Muggeridge. "You've been working here in these streets for eighteen years?"

"Yes," she said simply and yet joyfully. "It is my privilege to be here. These are my people. These are the ones my Lord has given me to love."

"Do you ever get tired? Do you ever feel like quitting and letting someone else take over your ministry? After all, you are beginning to get older."

"Oh, no," she replied, "this is where the Lord wants me, and this is where I am happy to be. I feel young when I am here. The Lord is so good to me. How privileged I am to serve him."

Later, Malcolm Muggeridge said, "I will never forget that little lady as long as I live. The face, the glow, the eyes, the love—it was all so pure and so beautiful. I shall never forget it. It was like being in the presence of an angel. It changed my life. I have not been the same person since. It is more than I can describe." By the way, after Malcolm Muggeridge made those comments, Mother Teresa continued to serve in that sacrificial way until the end of her life—nearly twenty-seven more years.

Obviously, we can't all be Mother Teresa but we *can* all live in that spirit. In our own ways, we can all be servants, we can all be witnesses. Like Mother Teresa, we live in the Spirit of Christ. To him we can COME and find Life. With him, we can WAIT and find strength. For him, we can GO and find places to serve.

Study Guide

Some Folks Feel the Rain...
Others Just Get Wet

Written by John D. Schroeder

This study guide is designed for both individual and group use. When using the book individually, you may choose to read the entire book and then revisit each chapter as you make your way through the study guide. Or, if you prefer, you may take one chapter at a time, reading a chapter and then considering the questions provided for that chapter. In either case, you will find it helpful to record your responses and reflections in a notebook or journal.

When using the book in a group, you may cover one chapter per session, or you may combine or select specific chapters as you choose to shorten your study. When combining two or more chapters for a given session, you may condense the material by selecting from the study questions provided.

Prior to your first session, determine who will serve as group leader. For this study, the leader's role is to facilitate discussion and encourage participation by all group members. To ensure fruitful discussion, *all participants* must commit to reading the designated chapter(s) before each group session. If open discussion is new or uncomfortable to your group, or if your time together is limited, it may be helpful for group members to reflect on the selected study questions prior to the session as well. Some may want to record their responses in a notebook or make brief notes in their books. (Note: Some questions may seem more appropriate for personal reflection than for group discussion. If members of your group are reluctant to discuss these questions, agree to reflect on them individually during the coming week.)

Remember, this is a study *guide*—intended to help lead you on an exploration of the book's primary themes and lessons. The "journey," however, will be different for each group or individual making it. Some will need to take a few detours; others will want to linger at times before moving ahead. Whether studying the book alone or with a group, feel free to adapt the questions as necessary to meet your particular needs and interests or those of your group. In addition to this book, you will need a Bible and a Bible concordance. Though it is not essential to your study, you may also find a Bible dictionary to be a helpful resource. (Groups will need only one Bible concordance and one Bible dictionary.) May God richly bless you through your study.

Introduction: Some Folks Feel the Rain . . .
Others Just Get Wet

1. What do you think is the meaning of the title of this book? Give some examples to support your answer.

2. Describe a time when you felt the rain; then recall a time when you just got wet.

3. Recall the time you first learned the difference between these approaches—the difference between *celebrating* life and *coping* with life.

4. Reflect on Psalm 118:24. In your own words, tell what the psalmist was trying to teach us with these words.

5. According to the author, what's so important about gratitude?

6. What are the benefits of having a sense of humor?

7. How do we develop a partnership with God?

8. What do you hope to learn from studying this book? How would you like for it to change your life?

Chapter 1: Can You Feel the Strength to Keep on Believing When It's Hard?

1. What new insights did you gain from reading this chapter?

2. Share a time when the wind was taken out of your sails. How did you feel? How did you cope? What helped you recover?

3. What can we learn from Jesus' actions toward Doubting Thomas? What does this mean for us today?

4. What is proof for you that something exists or that something did happen? How can our attitude limit what we believe?

5. Recall your feelings when you first heard about the Oklahoma City bombing. What were your first thoughts? What images come to mind now? What insights did this incident provide you with concerning death? concerning life?

6. Read John 20:24-29. What lessons can we learn from this passage? What does it tell us about Jesus? about bouncing back from defeat? about what it takes to believe?

7. Discuss a time when you were a Doubting Thomas— when you dropped out, wanted proof, or believed the end had come.

8. What changes a person into a Believing Thomas? Is it something from within or something from God?

9. List ways that God provides strength when life gets hard.

Chapter 2: Can You Feel the Zest of Life?

1. What new insights about the zest of life did you gain from reading this chapter? In your own words, what is the "zest of life"? What does having a zest for life mean to you?

2. Read 2 Corinthians 4:7-12 again. Give a summary of these verses and what they mean to you.

3. List ingredients that cause a person to have a zest for life. Can you have a zest for life without being a Christian? Explain your answer.

4. In your own words, define "prison shuffle." What numbs people and causes them to get caught in the prison shuffle?

5. Share a time in your life when you were caught in the "prison shuffle." What helped you escape, change, and become a different person?

6. What can you do to help another person escape from the prison shuffle in life, in faith, or in hard times? Are there any risks involved? If so, name some of them.

Chapter 3: Can You Feel the Power of Commitment?

1. What new insights did you gain from reading this chapter?

2. Discuss and list the benefits of walking in love, trust, and commitment. How would you define the power of commitment? What are the costs of making a commitment?

3. Recall a time when you were limping along in life or in a certain situation. How did the problem begin, and how did it end?

4. What causes people to start "limping"? How can people "limp" without knowing it?

5. What impressed you about the contest Elijah arranged between Baal and God?

6. When we stop "limping with two different opinions," what happens? How are we changed?

7. In your own words, explain this statement: "Faith is not believing without evidence, but trusting without reservation." In what ways is trust important in your life— for example, in your family relationships or your work relationships?

8. Describe someone you know who honors God by walking in love. What special traits or characteristics does this person have? In what ways is he or she an ordinary person? an extraordinary person?

Chapter 4: Can You Feel the Joy of Freedom?

1. What new insights did you gain from reading this chapter?

2. Read Matthew 25:14-18 again. Why did the servant with one talent act as he did? What do you think were his motivations? What can cause us to become like this servant? What causes a person to act like the servant with several talents?

3. What does the joy of freedom mean to you? Share a time when you experienced this freedom.

4. What does it mean to be frozen by our appetites? Give an example.

5. Name some things that can restrain us from achievement and doing our best.

6. Give some examples of being frozen by negative attitudes and crippling anxieties. List some strategies for feeling the joy of freedom.

7. What are the costs of freedom? What price do we need to pay? How does the freedom that God offers us in Jesus Christ differ from all other kinds of freedom?

Chapter 5: Can You Feel the Power of Love?

1. What new insights did you gain from reading this chapter?

2. How would you describe to someone else the power of love?

3. Share a time when you were a recipient of the power of love.

4. Read Acts 3:1-10. How can we get "the spirit of Jesus" to perform acts of love—good works in the example of Jesus? What is required of us?

5. In your own words, what qualifies for a miracle? Define it. What is necessary for a miracle to occur? Who can perform miracles? How are miracles and love related?

6. Have you ever been the recipient of—or witness to—a miracle? Share your story.

7. According to the author, what three things helped

Karen find the courage to perform her "miracle of love"?

8. Name some ways in which we can be miracle workers. How can we enable others to work miracles? If possible, give an example of a situation where one person's miracle spread out to others.

9. Name some words, attitudes, or actions that changed your life.

Chapter 6: Can You Feel the Strength to Persevere?

1. What new insights did you gain from reading this chapter?

2. Give an example of a time when you persevered and were glad you did. What motivated you? How did you feel at the end?

3. What does it cost to persevere? List the benefits of "hanging in there" and accomplishing an objective. How does accomplishment change a person?

4. What do we gain from regular church attendance? What can we miss through irregular attendance?

5. How have the Ten Commandments influenced your morality and caused you to persevere? Give some examples from throughout your life.

6. In what ways do people "reinvent the wheel" when it comes to salvation and morality? In what subtle ways are we encouraged—by other individuals and by society in general—to change?

7. Reread John 21:15-19. Why did Jesus repeat the words

"feed my sheep" to Peter three times? What was he telling Peter?

Chapter 7: Can You Feel the Attitude of Gratitude?

1. What new insights did you gain from reading this chapter?

2. Share an episode of grit, grace, or gratitude that you experienced. How did it change you?

3. Reread Luke 19:1-10. What do you think is the most amazing part of this story, and why? Why do you think Zacchaeus sought out Jesus? Do you think Zacchaeus remained a tax collector after this experience? Why or why not?

4. According to the author, what three ingredients are necessary for a life-changing experience? What others would you add?

5. Share a time when God gave you a second chance. How did you feel? How was your life changed?

6. In your own words, define *grit*. What are its risks and rewards? Why is it hard for some people to "say yes to God"?

7. What do you think is so amazing about grace? How would you explain grace to someone? How do you feel after receiving grace? Give an example.

8. What is the cause of gratitude? In what ways is gratitude expressed? How does a sense of gratitude change your life? List some different ways we can show gratitude to God and others.

Chapter 8: Can You Feel the Call to Discipleship?

1. What new insights did you gain from reading this chapter?

2. In your own words, explain discipleship—what it is, what it means to you, and how you become a disciple.

3. What does it mean to be "tired of clapping with one hand"? When have you felt this way? Give an example.

4. Where does emptiness come from? Why would someone with youth, power, and wealth still feel something is missing?

5. According to the author, what actions must we take in order to be happy, be excited about life, be full of zest and excitement, and make our life count for something?

6. In your own words, explain this statement: "We have to look higher than this world for our happiness." Complete this sentence: Real life is . . .

7. According to the author, Jesus' emphasis is not on the cost of discipleship, but on the riches of discipleship. In your life (or in the life of someone you know), what are the costs of discipleship? What are the riches of discipleship? How do the two compare?

8. What makes it so hard to prioritize? What are the results of not getting our priorities straight? What happens when we are able to get our priorities straight?

9. What happens when we are not able to love? What happens when we are not able to trust? Read John 13:34 and Proverbs 3:5-6; what do these passages say to us about love and trust?

Chapter 9: Can You Feel the Quality of Childlikeness?

1. What new insights did you gain from reading this chapter?

2. Do you have a favorite story from this chapter? If so, which one, and why?

3. What have you learned from children, and how has that knowledge changed your life?

4. In your own words, what is childlikeness? Name some qualities in children that are lacking in many adults.

5. In Mark 10:13-16, why did the disciples want the children to stay away? Why did Jesus want the children to come close to him? What does this story reveal about Jesus? about the disciples?

6. Why do we tend to glorify adulthood? How does the gospel reverse this?

7. Share a favorite childhood memory. Why do you treasure this memory?

8. What causes us to lose our childlike behavior? Can we get it back?

9. What one quality would you like to add to your life to be more childlike? Explain. Giving examples from your own life or from the lives of others you know, describe special or unique ways in which children have shown gratitude, love, and faith.

Chapter 10: Can You Feel the Firm Foundation?

1. What new insights did you gain from reading this chapter?

2. In your own words, define the "perfect" church.

3. What is a firm foundation? How do we build a firm foundation in our daily lives? at work? at church? What are the costs of building a firm foundation?

4. Give a summary of the spirit and mission of Christ as discussed in this chapter.

5. What are signs of a church having a firm foundation? signs of a church lacking a firm foundation?

6. Discuss the three "rocks" of the firm foundation—faith, hope, and love. Are there any other rocks that you would include? If so, name them and give an explanation for each one.

7. Why is the author sold on the church? List his reasons.

8. How did you select your church? What process did you go through? What were you looking for? What did you find?

Chapter 11: Can You Feel the Good Side of Worry?

1. What new insights did you gain from reading this chapter?

2. In your own words, explain the good side of worry; how does worry add to our lives? Then, explain the bad side of worry; how does worry detract from our lives?

3. Recall something that caused you to worry. What was the eventual outcome? Did worry help or hinder the situation?

4. List some strategies for handling worry. Rank them by importance. How many of these strategies can be found in the Bible?

5. Reread Matthew 6:25-34. What are the key points Jesus wants us to remember?

6. Why did God give us worry energy and anxiety energy? How can they be used to worry creatively or productively?

7. Explain or discuss this statement: Our worry list tells a lot about us and our priorities.

8. How can we direct our worry energy to the real priorities of life—toward matters that really matter? How can worry motivate us to positive action? Give examples. How can our worries bring us back to God? What must happen in order for this to occur?

9. In a sentence or a few words, what is the answer to worry?

Chapter 12: Can You Feel the New Way of Looking at Things?

1. What new insights did you gain from reading this chapter?

2. Share a time in your life when you were facing the wrong direction and missed a miracle or something important. How did you feel?

3. Respond to / discuss this statement: Religion is a way of seeing.

4. Reread Exodus 14:10-15. How is it that God, Moses, and the people all saw things differently? What is the message in this passage for us in our lives today?

5. What do we need in order to see things from a new per-

spective? How does God want us to look at life, others, and our situations?

6. In your own words, what does it mean to believe? What does the author say must first take place before we can believe? What role does faith play in our belief? What does our way of seeing things—the way we look at the world—have to do with belief?

7. What role does forgiveness play in our relationships with others? What happens to us when we make peace with others? What happens to the forgiven party?

8. What is the role of trust in our relationships with others? What happens when we trust someone? What is necessary in order for God to deliver us from our troubles?

Chapter 13: Can You Feel the Miracle of Encouragement?

1. What new insights did you gain from reading this chapter?

2. In your own words, define *encouragement*. Tell about an encouraging person you know.

3. Recall a time when someone gave you the gift of encouragement. Share the results and how you felt.

4. Give an example of when you offered encouragement to someone and how it helped. How did this giving make you feel?

5. What does the author mean when he is talking about "the miracle of encouragement"? From your own experience or from the life of someone you know, how does encouragement involve a miracle?

6. According to the author, what is the essential message of encouragement that we should spread, whether at church, at home, at school or elsewhere? Make a list of ways that Christians and the church can be instruments of encouragement. In what ways have you recently been an instrument of encouragement in your family? in your church? in your faith?

7. Are there any risks or costs involved in offering encouragement? Give some examples.

8. Reread Matthew 28:16-20. What kind of encouragement does Jesus promise? How does it differ from the encouragement we can offer to others?

Chapter 14: Can You Feel the Sense of What's Valuable?

1. What new insights did you gain from reading this chapter?

2. In your own words, give a summary of Paul's message in 1 Thessalonians 5:12-22. What are his main points? Why is this message so important for us today?

3. Do you have something that has little or no monetary value, but which you cherish nevertheless? What is it, and why is it valuable to you?

4. What makes something valuable? Give an example of something that may be valuable to one person, yet worthless to another.

5. How do we get a sense of what is valuable and what is worthless? How does the world confuse us about what is worthy and what is worthless? Who do we listen to regarding these judgments?

6. Read Psalm 146; Romans 5:1-5; 1 Peter 1:3; 1 John 3:2-3. What do these verses say about hope? about perseverance? about second chances? In your life, what gives you hope or inspires hope within you?

7. What are we to do with our spirit of gratitude, hope, and love? How can we make these three spirits grow?

8. Has anyone ever given you a gift of gratitude, hope, or love? Share your story and how the person or the situation made you feel.

Chapter 15: Can You Feel the Beauty of Inclusiveness?

1. What new insights did you gain from reading this chapter?

2. In your own words, explain the beauty of inclusiveness. Why is it so important that the author devoted an entire chapter to it?

3. Recall a time when you were excluded from a group or activity. How did you feel? What barrier kept you apart?

4. Reread Ephesians 2:13-22. What does the apostle Paul say about Jesus' role as a peacemaker? Locate and make a list of examples from the Gospels that show Jesus' words, attitudes, and actions toward inclusiveness, bridging differences, and bringing people together through kindness and love.

5. How is the church inclusive? Are there any ways it is not inclusive? What barriers exist?

6. List some ways that we as Christian individuals can be inclusive at home, at work, and in our daily activities. What prevents us from being inclusive?

7. In your own words, describe the two kinds of pride that the author mentions. What kind of pride do you have in your life right now? Does your pride bring you closer to other people or does it create barriers and separateness?

8. Define *prejudice*. Think about groups or individuals you are aware of who are excluded due to prejudice. Are there appropriate ways in which you can offer encouragement or work to effect positive change? How? What does the author say is the key to defeating prejudice?

9. What does the author say about vengeance? Read Matthew 18:21-22. What does Jesus tell us about forgiveness? Who does forgiveness benefit the most—the one who gives it or the one who receives it?

10. What are the benefits of being inclusive? What are the costs?

Epilogue: Can You Feel God Hugging You to Life?

1. What new insights did you gain from reading this chapter?

2. In what ways does God hug us to life?

3. Share a time when you got so caught up in something that you forgot something important, forgot where you were going, forgot the core of your faith. How were you reminded? How did you feel?

4. Discuss *come*, the call to life. Who calls us, and why?

5. Discuss *wait*, the call to worship. Why is this so

important? What are the risks we face by ignoring this command?

6. Discuss *go*, the call to service. What types of service are we called to perform as Christians? Of the three commands, which is the hardest for you to follow, and why?

7. How has this book affected your life? What did you learn? Have you changed? How? What impressed you? Are there any chapters that stand out for you?